WHITE
HOUSES

WHITE HOUSES

PHILIP JODIDIO

260+ illustrations

Thames & Hudson

CONTENTS

White homes can be found all over the world, from the traditional houses of Mykonos and Santorini in Greece, to the pristine Villa Savoye by Le Corbusier (Poissy, France, 1931), or the almost obsessional work of Richard Meier in the United States. This book is a tour of the world from Australia to Brazil, highlighting not only the far-flung reach of modern whiteness, but also the ways in which architects play on shadow and reflected colours to bring their often angular white designs to life.

The whiteness of snow or clouds, and on occasion the unfiltered light of the sun, shows that white architecture is by no means entirely artificial. White is defined sometimes as an absence of colour, but in fact a white surface reflects light of all hues completely and diffusely. In this it is the sum of colours, the reflected purity of the entire spectrum. White is associated with purity in religions from Christianity to Shinto, but in some cultures also with mourning. It is the colour of the new, of beginnings, but also of imagined ghosts and spirits. And then it can be the colour of the flag of surrender. White is everywhere.

WHITE IS THE LIGHT

TO THE EDGE OF SENSORY DEPRIVATION

Surely influenced by Le Corbusier, Richard Meier became the white knight of modern architecture, beginning in the early 1970s with such works as the Douglas House (Harbor Springs, Michigan, 1973), which was widely published at the time. But whiteness was not to the taste of all. Thinking perhaps of the Douglas House, Tom Wolfe, in his tongue-in-cheek 1981 opus *From Bauhaus to Our House*, wrote: 'Every new $900,000 summer house in the north woods of Michigan or on the shore of Long Island has so many pipe railings, ramps, hob-tread metal spiral stairways, sheets of industrial plate glass, banks of tungsten-halogen lamps and white cylindrical shapes, it looks like an insecticide refinery. I once saw the owners of such a place driven to the edge of sensory deprivation by the whiteness & lightness & leanness & cleanness & bareness & spareness of it all. They became desperate for an antidote, such as coziness and color.'[1] Meier himself reacted to this indictment in his acceptance speech for the 1984 Pritzker Prize, stating: 'And I have to explain that for me, white is the most wonderful color because within it you can see all the colors of the rainbow. For me, in fact it is the color which in natural light, reflects and intensifies the perception of all the shades of the rainbow, the colors which are constantly changing in nature, for whiteness of white is never just white; it is almost always transformed by light and that which is changing; the sky, the clouds, the sun and the moon.'[2]

Although Richard Meier continues to create white mansions on green hills such as the Oxfordshire Residence (2017, page 34), the interest of these exchanges about the virtues of whiteness can be found in the underlying facts. Cultural and traditional in some countries, such as Portugal and Greece, white houses today embody the brightness and cleanliness that remain associated with modernity. If any architectural volume can be at once assertive and still make way for the observation of nature and the propagation of light, then white it should be.

Page 7 House in Leiria, Leiria, Portugal, 2011, Aires Mateus. The architects fashion pure white forms in a manner that approaches minimalist art.

Above Mosha House, Tehran, Iran, 2016, New Wave Architecture. A composition of stacked boxes, this house contrasts white surfaces and wood in its interior spaces.

THE APPEAL OF NOTHINGNESS

The artist Wassily Kandinsky wrote of the symbolic value of colours in his seminal text *Concerning the Spiritual in Art* (1910). 'White,' he said, 'has this harmony of silence, that works upon us in a negative way, like many pauses in music that temporarily break the melody. It is not a dead silence, but one pregnant with possibilities. White has the appeal of the nothingness that is before birth, of the world in the ice age … Not without reason is white taken as symbolizing joy and spotless purity, and black grief and death.' In a different mode, in the New Testament, white is the colour of the Transfiguration: 'After six days Jesus took Peter, James and John with him and led them up a high mountain, where they were all alone. There he was transfigured before them. His clothes became dazzling white, whiter than anyone in the world could bleach them' (Mark 9:2–3). Though white is a colour of mourning in certain cultures, it is worn by Hajj pilgrims in Islam, and, in the Jewish world, by rabbis at Yom Kippur.

OF CATHEDRALS AND GODS

The powerful association of white with modern art can be seen in such early works as *Suprematist Composition: White on White* (1918) by Kazimir Malevich, but also in the 'white cube' style of art gallery, pioneered by New York's Museum of Modern Art (MoMA) under Alfred Barr in the 1930s. In modern architecture, it was in part thanks to Le Corbusier that 'white' in a figurative sense became a symbol of the new. In 1947, he wrote: 'The new world was beginning. White, limpid, joyous, clean, clear and without hesitations, the new world was opening up like a flower among the ruins. They left behind them all recognized ways of doing things, they turned their backs on all that. In a hundred years, the marvel was accomplished and Europe was changed. The cathedrals were white.'[3] It is of little (symbolic) importance that the cathedrals were in fact not white when they were built; rather it is Le Corbusier's insistence on the 'white, limpid, joyous, clean, clear…' architecture of the 'new world' that can be noted. Nor was 'Corbu' the only proponent of colourless purity in modern architecture. Ludwig Mies van der Rohe is one of several Bauhaus figures who went on to have considerable influence on the evolution of architecture and art in America. Tom Wolfe impishly baptized this group, which included Walter Gropius, Marcel Breuer and Josef Albers, the White Gods. The Farnsworth House by Mies (Plano, Illinois, 1951) remains a quintessential expression of Modernism, its exposed structural steel painted pristine white.

It is not a coincidence that a group of five New York architects (Peter Eisenman, Michael Graves, Charles Gwathmey, John Hejduk and Richard Meier) who identified themselves in the early 1970s with abstraction and purism came to be called the Whites. Meier has certainly proven to be the strongest defender of the symbolic importance of whiteness in contemporary architecture. In explaining his use of white cladding, Meier verges on a philosophical approach, which may well have something to do with the frequency of this shade in much contemporary architecture. 'White,' he has stated, 'is the ephemeral emblem of perpetual movement.

The white is always present but never the same, bright and rolling in the day, silver and effervescent under the full moon of New Year's Eve. Between the sea of consciousness and earth's vast materiality lies this ever-changing line of white. *White is the light*, the medium of understanding and transformative power.'[4]

A MUTABLE PRESENCE

The symbolic import of white architecture seems to have diminished as Modernism has faded in the collective memory. And yet white, that beam of light that Isaac Newton first passed through a prism in 1665, discovering what he identified as seven constituent colours, is, if anything, more and more present in new buildings. Because a white wall is most capable of assuming the shades of its environment, from forest green to sky blue, white is seen less as an immutable value than as a mutable presence. White is still the colour most associated with purity and cleanliness: from bathroom tiles to gleaming teeth, perfection is spotlessly white. In architecture, what colour stands out from its environment better than an absence of other shades? More recently than Modernism, minimalism in the hands of such able practitioners as John Pawson has also readily been dressed in white. The English architect made admirable use of white, for example in his remodelling of the St Moritz Church (Augsburg, Germany, 2013), where the utilization of light and the resultant creation of a nearly immaterial presence are mediated by white surfaces.

Below MM House, Palma de Mallorca, Spain, 2016, OHLAB. White walls and an old piece of furniture contrast with the beige and green tile floor, which provides radiant heating and cooling.

TOMB OF LIGHT

In unexpected ways, white can be seen as an affirmation of presence, the formation of a distinct outline against an otherwise variegated background, but also as an expression of absence, or even quasi-invisibility. The aptly named Ghost House (Jin Otagiri, Tokyo, 2005, page 138) seems to be no more than the form of a house, with no visible windows and an interior where white-on-white made the *Financial Times* comment that 'It could be Zen; it could be sensory deprivation'. The architect, Jin Otagiri, called it both 'one of the most minimalist houses in Japan' and an 'archetypical primitive hut-like house'. The double sloped-roof form of the house is indeed relatively 'archetypical' but this Ghost House also signifies a kind of transition from the crowded reality of Tokyo to the emptiness of white. In their comprehensive *Dictionnaire des Symboles*, Jean Chevalier and Alain Gheerbrant state: 'Like its opposite, black, white can be situated at either end of the chromatic range. Absolute and having no variations but those that go from matte to brilliant, white can signify absence, or at the other extreme, the sum of all colours. White is thus placed alternatively at the beginning and at the end of daily life and the manifest world, which grants it an asymptotic, ideal value. But the end of life – the moment of death – is also a moment of transition, at the juncture of the visible and the invisible, and thus at a new point of departure.'[5] The Ghost House also has a tomb-like quality, albeit a tomb that is filled with light.

Another Japanese residence published here, the White Cave House (Takuro Yamamoto, Kanazawa, 2013, page 160), tends to a kind of absolute simplicity

characterized by an absence of visible openings and pervasive whiteness. Built in a region known for its winter snowfalls, the White Cave provides shelter from the elements almost by way of melting into its environment. And what an unexpected idea to colour a 'cave' white, a kind of pristine womb, or again, perhaps a place of transition from this world to the next.

In a more humorous vein, the Canadian architects Delordinaire created their surprising High House (Saint-Ferréol-les-Neiges, Quebec, 2017, page 16) in the midst of a field often covered with snow. Here the nearly archetypical form of a house is unexpectedly raised up on stilts, floating above the snow but also blending into it entirely in the winter months. In this environment, the usually bold contrast between white architecture and nature dissolves at least for part of the year.

In countries where white architecture has always been present, a number of contemporary architects play on this tradition to assert a different kind of modernity, not forcibly related to Modernism. With their House in Leiria (Portugal, 2011, page 122), Aires Mateus play on the form of a typical house, while leaving all of its visible surfaces, including the roof, entirely white. As is the case for their Japanese counterparts, the Portuguese architects chose this solution not for any radical aesthetic reason so much as to provide complete privacy for the owners in a 'chaotic' neighbourhood environment. It is true that the crisp white forms of the house make it stand out in a very visible fashion, while its nearly complete closure frustrates outside curiosity entirely. There is no denying that this is a house, but its white impermeability signals that beyond its surface, all that lies within is private.

CASTLES BY THE SEA

Two other, larger houses on the Iberian Peninsula published in this volume speak to a different image of whiteness, the Casa Elíptica (Luz, Lagos, Portugal, 2014, page 260) by Mário Martins and the Cliff House (Calpe, Alicante, Spain, 2012, page 266) by Fran Silvestre. The 242-square-metre (2,605 sq ft) Cliff House is meant to be 'a house on the air, walking on water', while the 400-square-metre (4,300 sq ft) Casa Elíptica also overlooks the water, laid out under a great cantilevered elliptical form that was imagined as though it had been carved out by the wind. In some sense these are white castles hovering above the sea, offering the promise of an eternity once again perceived in nature. The whiteness and geometric purity here is a step closer to heaven, or in a less religious mode, to the infinite.

The Summer House (Oia, Santorini, 2017, page 252) by the Greek architect Alexandros Kapsimalis also represents a modern take on the houses of Santorini and was based on an existing 'cave house' set above the waters of the Aegean Sea. Sprayed concrete (gunite) was used to affirm the amorphous curvature of interior spaces, here once again imagining a cave as a luminous white space. With such elements as a cantilevered infinity pool signifying its modernity, this house nonetheless was literally built on the foundations of already white local architecture.

In other locations, the use of pristine white can be in contrast to existing architecture, thereby offering an interpretation of tradition that can readily be distinguished from older buildings. An example of this type of variation on the theme of whiteness can be seen with the House at Maghera by McGonigle McGrath (Northern Ireland, 2014, page 108). Referencing typical local architecture and its pitched slate or steel roofs, the architects nonetheless opt for modern white forms.

ALWAYS PRESENT BUT NEVER THE SAME

It would seem clear that no colour, not even black, is as replete with symbolic or historic meanings as white. One is tempted to imagine the white-robed Christ of the Transfiguration declaring, 'I am the Alpha and the Omega, the First and the Last, the Beginning and the End' – though of course the white of architecture need not be religious. 'White, limpid, joyous, clean, clear and without hesitations', the new world of architecture is again and always white. Like a blank sheet of paper, or a painter's untouched canvas, white walls are an invitation to the reflected colours of their surroundings and the changing light of day. More than any colour, white is capable of flowing, continual and subtle change in appearance, borne by shadows, the sky or a nearby tree. For some architects and indeed some of their clients, a white environment is forcibly imbued with modernity and may too evoke an accessible form of eternity, an invitation to the white light of transition. A white house can be a statement, translating a desire to stand out, just as it can be designed to be neutral or blank. Whiteness can be used to press the frontiers of form to the point of abstraction, and ultimately dissolution.

1. Tom Wolfe, *From Bauhaus to Our House*, Farrar Straus Giroux, New York, 1981
2. Richard Meier, 1984 Pritzker Prize acceptance speech, www.pritzkerprize.com/1984/ceremony_speech1, accessed on 20 July 2017
3. Le Corbusier, *Quand les Cathédrales étaient blanches* (1947), translated by Francis E. Hyslop, McGraw Hill, New York, 1964, page 4
4. Richard Meier in *Richard Meier Architect, 1985/1991*, Rizzoli, New York, 1991
5. Jean Chevalier, Alain Gheerbrant, *Dictionnaire des Symboles*, Robert Laffont/Jupiter, Paris, 1968, page 125, translated by the author

MM House, Palma de Mallorca, Spain, 2016, OHLAB. The white exterior composition of the house is sharply defined against the evening sky.

SCULPTURES

FOR

LANDSCAPES

There is something about geometric white forms that speaks the language of contemporary art and sculpture — a white slashed canvas by Lucio Fontana, a *White Curve* by Ellsworth Kelly. White was a preferred tone of Le Corbusier, and also in more recent years of Richard Meier, who is present here with his Oxfordshire Residence (page 34). The High House of Delordinaire (page 16) sits above its often white landscape like a disembodied object, while the AA House by Carlos Ferrater (page 20) immediately brings to mind a purely geometric work of white-paper origami. Some contemporary architects actively explore the idea of buildings that resemble nothing so much as pure abstract sculptures, where usual features of buildings from a visible roof to windows are not necessarily visible. This is the case with the Sugarcubes house by Montenegro Architects (page 40). The Haus am Weinberg (UNStudio, page 58) is a sculpture of another sort, with curving forms that express the language of computer-assisted design.

DELORDINAIRE

/

HIGH

HOUSE

\

CANADA

This unusual house is literally lifted up off the ground on stilts. To some extent, it brings to mind Herzog & de Meuron's renowned Rudin House (Leymen, France, 1997), built of concrete and poised on slender pillars. The 90-square-metre (970 sq ft) residence sits so high that it leaves room for an outdoor stove at ground level. In this way, and despite the cold winters of this site not far from Quebec City, it 'plays with the limit between interior and exterior, inviting people to gather in spaces immersed in nature', according to the architects. The white colouring obtained using concrete panels blends the structure into the snowy environment; in warmer months it stands out against the countryside.

The positioning of the house on stilts makes its 'footprint', in both literal and environmental terms, less significant. The stilts required a minimal amount of excavation, and can be removed with little work should the house be moved or demolished. A partial cantilever enlivens the form that is otherwise very reminiscent of the outlines of a 'typical' house. The living areas, aside from the covered outdoor space at ground level, are on the single upper storey, where two bedrooms, one bathroom, the kitchen and the living space are concentrated.

Page 14 Sugarcubes, Grândola, Tróia, Portugal, 2014, Montenegro Architects. Strict white lines reveal little of the internal disposition of the residence.

Pages 16-17 The house appears to be a 'normal' structure except for the fact that it is lifted high above the ground, with only an inclined ladder and thin pilotis touching the earth.

Right A pine grid forms the structure of the main large window that wraps around the end of the house (visible from the exterior, opposite).

Opposite The image of a flying or hovering house has rarely been integrated into an architectural design in this way, although there are some precedents.

OAB –

CARLOS

FERRATER

PARTNERSHIP

/

AA HOUSE

\

SPAIN

Designed by Carlos Ferrater and Xavier Marti, this unusual, large (1,500 square metre / 16,146 sq ft) residence is located in Sant Cugat del Vallès, a town located north of the centre of Barcelona. Described by the architects as a 'boat anchored in a green sea of grass', it is situated near a golf course at the edge of a forest. The designers compare the four narrow, almost hidden staircases in the building to those on a boat. A loft where the client keeps a collection of maps is reached via a folding ladder. Inspired by the forms of origami ('like a temporary Japanese pavilion') this project has also been called the Origami House and, according to Ferrater, its sources of inspiration range from Louis Kahn to Alison and Peter Smithson and Charles and Ray Eames. The white forms of the residence make the reference to origami entirely clear. The 7 x 7 m (23 x 23 ft) orthogonal floor plan gives way to 45° inclined volumes that are visible in section drawings, and which are intended to offer views of the garden and broader landscape of the site. The diagonal forms also generate double-height spaces and skylights, creating the 'artificial topography' of the roofscape. The kitchen is likened to a house in itself, 'a world opened completely onto the garden and bathed in natural daylight, a systematic laboratory of nutrition, care, cleaning and work'. A collection of cars is stored in the lower-level garage. The architects state: 'This is a house and it is the contrary: telluric and anchored at the base, and yet light and floating like a balloon about to leave the ground. It takes us back to the idea of a "house" as an authentic archetype as understood by Gaston Bachelard and Luis Barragán: with a basement and an attic. With all of its intensity and meaning, this house contains all the symbols. It is a house on pleasant land, all garden, which floats above the grass.'

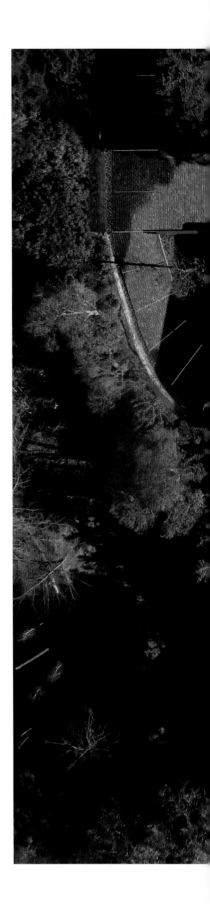

Pages 20-21 The garden-side elevation of the house has full-height glazing that reveals a generous library/office and the living spaces. A single tree marks the patio.

Right An aerial view shows the plan of the building and also the marked resemblance to a kind of Japanese origami or folded-paper design.

Below The entrance façade is
largely closed and does not reveal
the height of some of the volumes.
A water feature and black stone
contrast with the whiteness of
the house.

Opposite The angled roof design
creates double-height, glazed
façades on the more private side
of the house.

Overleaf The central living space
opens almost entirely to the
garden. The white design seems to
correspond well to the feeling of
spatial freedom generated by this
configuration.

JOÃO

MENDES

RIBEIRO

/

FONTE

BOA

HOUSE

\

PORTUGAL

The Fonte Boa House is a 180-square-metre (1,940 sq ft) single-family residence located on the western part of a rural estate in Fartosa, Fonte Boa, in the centre of Portugal, south of Coimbra, where the architect is based. The small estate includes a vineyard and an olive grove. Construction preserved the surrounding trees and maintained the existing slope of the site.

The house is a two-storey rectangular structure with a pitched, zinc-covered roof, and has a concrete basement level that is used as a wine cellar. On the ground floor, a stairway and utility area divide the living and dining room, while the two main bedrooms are located on the upper level. Windows of different sizes are used to create a 'connection' between the house and the landscape. Concrete and stone walls mark a progression towards the house, which is otherwise placed quite simply among the olive trees. The white simplicity of the house contrasts with the natural, farm environment, but its openings ensure that it is in harmony with its location.

Pages 28-29 The house is set up on a concrete block to avoid undue excavation of the sloped site. It contrasts strongly with the natural farmland environment, but its windows offer numerous views of the setting.

Above Basically a white rectangular volume, the house stands out crisply from its natural hillside environment.

Opposite Wooden stairs with built-in drawers rise to the second level without any handrail. Windows connect the strictly designed interior spaces with views of the farmland site.

Left A glass box creates a
transition between the exterior
and the inside of the house,
bringing natural light to
the area.

Right External concrete walls
mark the entrance to the house,
offering another point of contrast
with the main part of the structure
and the green site.

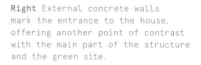

Above The sparsely furnished
interior of the living room
has full-height glazing, which
places residents 'in' the view
to some extent.

RICHARD

MEIER

/

OXFORDSHIRE

RESIDENCE

\

UK

Built to best take advantage of views of the countryside, the Oxfordshire Residence displays many of the characteristics of Richard Meier's architecture, including a geometric composition and overall whiteness. The scheme seeks to connect to the place and its history but also to make a statement in favour of sustainability. Meier seems quite comfortable with the tradition of the English manor house, even in the context of this pronounced modernity. Here there is not a curve in sight; the plan and elevations of the house are conceived in the spirit of untrammelled rectilinearity, careful compositions made up essentially of rectangles. The rear of the house, facing forest land, is closed, as often Meier's houses are even when placed near a road. The open landscape in front, however, invokes generous openings, and here, even a staircase can be the venue for a dramatic full-height view of the green surroundings.

The architect states: 'The house is anchored to its site, and has been carefully designed based on the human scale, the purity of the aesthetic, peerless construction methods and materials, and the conservation and utilization of natural resources.' Rather than seeing white as being in opposition to a natural setting, the architect clearly sees this absence of colour as the quintessence of light. The play on views but also on the natural light that reflects off the surfaces of the house and penetrates its volumes is proof of the continued mastery of Richard Meier. Although Meier participated in a Canary Wharf competition for an office building (1999) and the consultation for the US Embassy in London (2010), the Oxfordshire Residence is his first completed work in England.

Pages 34–35 Metal louvres hanging from the flat roof shield the living space from direct sunlight. The composition, as much as the white colour, is typical of Meier's style.

Opposite, above Sitting at the top of a hill, the house belies its rather considerable size with a sophisticated alternation of opaque white and transparent surfaces.

Opposite, below The rear façade of the building is naturally more closed than the garden elevation, a contrast that occurs frequently in Richard Meier's houses.

Above The double-height living room has an almost entirely transparent façade. Only the wooden floors contrast with the otherwise wholly white composition.

Opposite A detail view looking up into the louvres on the south side of the Oxfordshire Residence.

MONTENEGRO

ARCHITECTS

/

SUGARCUBES

\

PORTUGAL

This project involves a group of six houses located near the Troia golf course on the Troia peninsula, close to the Atlantic coast of southern Portugal. The architect has used variants on the same abstract, geometric white volumes to create unique residences. Seen from some outside angles, the houses seem to be a somewhat enigmatic collection of blank, angled blocks, whose whiteness contrasts markedly with the green of the natural environment. There is no clearly defined boundary between the domain of the houses and the surrounding garden terrain, contributing to a sense of freedom and connection to the site.

Though the designs are rectilinear they are not comprised of specific rectangular or even cubic forms, as the name Sugarcubes would imply – rather they make up a fairly intricate composition that can best be understood in plan drawings. The houses vary in size but have three levels, one of which is partially below grade. They thus share an obvious luminosity emphasized by the white surfaces inside and out, but appear to be smaller than they are.

Pages 40-41 Set among lavender and pines, the white forms of the house stand out in a sculptural way, making the functions of the building difficult to discern from the outside.

Left Sunlight and shadows create an abstract tableau where white surfaces contrast with the bright blue skies.

Right A passage between volumes recalls more traditional houses, although the crisp white and black lines of the design remain resolutely minimalist.

Below The rear elevations of the house offer staggered black-framed windows that contrast with otherwise blank white walls.

Opposite Inside the house, white surfaces and black frames are highlighted by light-coloured wood flooring, full-height glazing and a stairway that seems to float in space.

MU

ARCHITECTURE

/

THE

NOOK

\

CANADA

This 279-square-metre (3,000 sq ft) house is in Mansonville in the Eastern Townships of Quebec, on Lake Memphremagog and not far from the United States border and Vermont. It has a nearly blank façade on the street side, but to the rear the living space offers different views of the lake. A relaxation and contemplation space in the form of a sunken lounge separates public from private parts of the house.

According to the architects, the sloping site 'quickly dictated the first project constraints. The house clings to the steep terrain and seems to be projecting toward the lake. Like an origami, the two volumes are linked by a dynamic bending ribbon that merges the roofs together.' The projections of the roof provide shading and protect a large terrace that faces south. Exteriors are in white-painted pine, while indoors the house has polished concrete radiant floors, black ceramic tiles and walnut furniture. The ground floor has two large bedrooms, a bathroom and a dorm area; the upper level, with its open living space, is cantilevered over this volume.

Cedar ceilings extend outside along the roof soffits, emphasizing the architects' desire to create as much continuity between inside and out as possible in an often cold climate. In winter, the house blends readily into a snowy background and from inside, the generous glazing gives a real impression of proximity to nature. Although the basic plan of the house is entirely rectilinear, its angles and intersecting volumes provide spatial variety and enhance the play on views proposed by the architects.

Pages 46-47 The warm colours of the interior contrast with the house's white exterior and with the snowy environment. A slight cantilever of the upper level sits above the partially buried ground floor.

Right Simple furniture and a wood-burning stove are set off by a pine ceiling, a polished concrete floor and full-height glazing that gives a broad perspective of the area.

Right The dining area maintains the simplicity of the rest of the interior areas, with a table for eight, hanging lamps and full-height glazing.

Below The kitchen offers a black contrast to the lighter colours of the living area.

Opposite, above In the bedroom, lightweight metal bunk beds for children are placed above the beds of the parents.

Opposite, below The bathroom contrasts black tiles with a white sink and a white bathtub in front of a window. A glass wall separates the bath and shower area from the sink space.

NEW

WAVE

ARCHITECTURE

/

MOSHA

HOUSE

\

IRAN

Located in the north of Tehran, the Mosha House, which was designed in 2009, seven years before its completion, has a floor area of 260 square metres (2,800 sq ft). The architects explain that they opted for a 'vertical distribution of functions' in order to allocate more of the site to landscape on the sloped lot. Three cantilevered and rotated boxes were designed to create terraces and to provide panoramic views. The floor-to-ceiling windows on the sides of the boxes that face the Mosha plain 'are like a transparent curtain between inside and out' where natural views flow inside. This concept is confirmed by the use of wood on walls and floors and for the stairway. An inclined cylindrical shaft that encloses a spiral staircase links the boxes.

The designers explain that the white surfaces of the building that form a 'single white shield' preserve its 'purity' and make it stand out as a distinctive volume in the mountainous landscape. The house's somewhat jumbled forms might also bring to mind the fact that the potential for seismic activity in this zone is high. This house is certainly unusual in both its angled appearance and its obvious conception around views and openings that are contrasted with white closed surfaces. Despite being relatively cut off from the international architecture scene, Iran has consistently created interesting modern buildings.

Pages 52-53 The white, angled forms of the house with their glazed openings face in different directions, giving residents subtly varying views.

Opposite, above The overhanging volumes offer sheltered space with spectacular views of the mountains near Tehran in the distance.

Opposite, below Inside the house a pool room with a wooden deck has a full-height opening that frames the folding forms of the Alborz mountain range.

Above The floors and cabinets of the kitchen are formed with pine boards that contrast with the otherwise smooth, white surfaces.

Opposite A spiral staircase in raw pine connects the different levels of the residence, again offering a certain warmth in contrast to the whiteness of the walls.

UNSTUDIO

/

HAUS

AM

WEINBERG

\

GERMANY

This house is located on a hillside between a vineyard on one side and the city on the other. The Haus am Weinberg was designed with what the architects call a 'twist' that organizes the interiors of the residence around a central staircase. This gesture allows the architects to divide interior areas according to the required level of privacy or activities concerned. With full glazing at the four corners of the structure, daylight is brought in and views of the surroundings become an important feature.

Inside the house, in contrast with the dominant whiteness of the outside, natural oak flooring and stone are paired with white clay stucco with bits of reflective stone in the mixture. The project includes a number of custom-made furnishings. A white kitchen table/work surface extends from the kitchen towards the garden terrace, 'mimicking the curves in the architecture and further accentuating the connection between the inside and the outside'. A dark-wood multipurpose room contrasts with the otherwise largely white interiors. The south level contains the entrance hall, a garage, a wine cellar and a guest suite, as well as a diagonal staircase leading upstairs. A double-height glazed corner here was designed for the dining area, while the living room is near the corner that looks southwest. A second-floor gallery space is near the master bedroom suite and a wellness area.

The garden is intended in a sense to extend the masses and functions of the house to the exterior. The architect adds: 'The organization of the villa and the arrangement of movement flows and views are designed to imitate the strata of the surrounding landscape – and from the upper levels, of the surrounding cityscape – and thereby create an almost virtual experience of the landscape and the views from within the villa.'

Pages 58-59 The undulating white walls of the house give way to broad stretches of glazing. The combination of the two creates a sculptural form.

Left The large dining table sits on the lower level in a vast double-height space. The sloping site rises up beyond the glass walls, which also provide a view of the pool.

Below Echoing the exterior forms of the house, the sinuous white stairway winds up to the second level. The overall whiteness of the house is attenuated by the wooden floors and stairs.

Above The architects carefully
designed the entire house, including
the bathroom, where white surfaces
and a wooden floor emphasize the
overall continuity of the project.

STUDIO

RAZAVI

/

HOUSE

FOR

A

PHOTOGRAPHER

\

FRANCE

Loctudy is a picturesque fishing village located near Quimper in southern Brittany. The House for a Photographer, a 98-square-metre (1,055 sq ft) summer house and studio, is all the more surprising in this generally quite traditional, or strongly regional, architectural environment. The design is formed like a sort of stylized 'P', with one block for work and another for living space. On a restricted site, the house has openings only to the south and the east, otherwise offering blank white façades.

The sloping roof allows for a double-height living area and a mezzanine space for beds. Bathroom and bedroom areas are restricted in order to provide more living and working space. The architect states: 'The varying angles at the edges of the building offer a series of changing volumetric and perspective experiences, as is the case for the south façade that appears as a single vertical plane, while the other façades are hidden from view. Similarly an open angle in the main corridor undermines natural perspective to create an illusion of parallel walls.' Interior decor is minimal, in keeping with the white forms of the house itself. An outdoor terrace allows residents to take in the natural field environment.

Pages 64–65 The angular white volume of the house stands out against the background of its farmland site.

Opposite, above Apart from a band of grass on two sides, the house is placed almost directly in the natural prairie-like site.

Opposite, bottom The house differs considerably from its few neighbouring sloped-roof residences. The irregular window placement also differentiates it from the more traditional structures.

Opposite The white exterior of the house is carried over inside, to the white walls and ceilings. Light grey stone floors contrast to some extent with this monochromatic approach.

Above Vertical light tubes complement the abundant natural light in this hallway, where the exterior angles of the residence are also echoed.

NEW ANGLES

If white has long been considered the pre-eminent colour of modern design, in the hands of today's architects it takes many new and unexpected forms, from minimal geometric compositions to more exuberant shapes such as those employed in South Korea by HyoMan Kim (Flying House, page 72). Whether it be in joining a modern volume to an old house, as Matt Gibson does in Melbourne (Shakin' Stevens House, page 90), or in creating what appears to be an entirely new concept for the home (Jakob + MacFarlane, Connected House, page 98), white remains the reference, the baseline of all that is new. J. Mayer H., known for the swirling curves of works such as Metropol Parasol (Seville, Spain, 2011), calls on a stark contrast between white volumes and black window frames for the Dupli. Casa (page 102). Crisp white angles can be somewhat austere, as in the House at Maghera (McGonigle McGrath, page 108), or airy and light, as in the Villa Di Gioia (Pedone Working, page 114), but white walls always absorb and assume the colour of natural light, changing as the clock advances and the weather changes.

HYOMAN

KIM

/

IROJE

KHM

/

FLYING

HOUSE

\

SOUTH

KOREA

HyoMan Kim, the principal of IROJE KHM Architects, is searching for a Korean approach to contemporary architecture. 'Concept is an ideal and abstract thought,' he says. 'The concept does not hold value until it is embodied in a concrete building in reality.'

With a floor area of 195 square metres (2,100 sq ft), this residence sits on a small site (292 square metres/3,143 sq ft) located near Incheon International Airport. The owner of the house is a pilot. The architect states: 'We translated the pilot's lifestyle into an expression of the ... character of the traditional architecture of Korea.' A sunken sitting area (*ondol*), defined in keeping with the client's desire to be seated on the floor in the Korean manner, becomes in the hands of the architect a contemporary interpretation of an old residential principle. Similarly, the roof of the traditional garden pavilion (*rumaru*) is expressed by the 'dynamic concave curved outlines of the mass of the house'.

The main material used for the exterior is Dryvit, an inexpensive external wall insulation and finishing material, while the structure is made with concrete *ramen* (rigid walls) and exposed concrete blocks. White surfaces and forms dominate the design. Inside, the floors are in exposed concrete, and vinyl paint was used on the walls. The architect goes so far as to say that he hopes that the house will be recognized not as a piece of architecture but as a 'landscape in this village'.

Page 70 In the Villa Di Gioia (Bisceglie, Italy, 2011, Pedone Working), a white stair alternates opaque and light-filled effects in an abstract composition.

Pages 72-73 HyoMan Kim and IROJE KHM have developed an unexpected vocabulary that is at the same time related to Korean tradition and stunningly modern.

Opposite An airy pergola marks an outside terrace area in the uncompromisingly white house, which is surprising in almost every respect.

Below The main living space uses a geometric composition to link different levels and to create undefined areas that can be used in various ways.

Above Irregularity meets rectilinear design in this living area and interior balcony and passageway.

Opposite Grey metal contrasts with the dominant white in this stairway with a desk inserted into its lowest steps.

CHRIST.

CHRIST.

ASSOCIATED

ARCHITECTS

/

HOUSE

S

\

GERMANY

House S was originally a modern-style bungalow built by the interior architect Wilfried Hilger in the 1960s. New owners decided to raise the height of the original structure and to renovate the house. The Wiesbaden architect Roger Christ placed three box-like forms connected by a glass corridor on a cantilevered flat roof. One of the new boxes contains the master bedroom, dressing room and bath. The two other boxes function as a living room and home office. In the original structure, on the first floor, nearly all the walls were removed, allowing the creation of a large living space and open kitchen. Children's rooms, a dressing area and a bathroom were also inserted here. A guest room and an additional apartment are located on the ground floor.

Triple-glazed windows were used to reduce energy consumption. Fair-face concrete, rough-cut wood, white lacquered wood and Pilkington Profilit glass were used, and the building was clad in plaster, glass and rough oak. The 452-square-metre (4,865 sq ft) house sits on an 873-square-metre (9,400 sq ft) site. The overall effect of the building is one of rather minimal modernity, with open spaces and ample natural light.

Pages 78-79 White pilotis support the roof slab and partially cover a wooden terrace. Though its geometry is strict, the house projects an image of lightness.

Right A sliding glass wall connects the living space to a partially enclosed patio that is marked by a Japanese-style tree and stone composition.

Opposite Although it lacks protective barriers, the upper level planted roof serves as extra seating space in warm weather.

Above Seen from above, the house stands out from neighbouring residences but succeeds in creating a private realm, where whiteness rules.

EVELOP

ARQUITECTURA

/

CASA

S1

\

MEXICO

The 205-square-metre (2,205 sq ft) Casa S1 is in Zibatá, Querétaro, to the northwest of Mexico City. The architects place a certain emphasis on the contrast between the intimate private spaces for the clients – a young couple – and the more open social or public area. The entrance space, where there is a covered parking area for two cars, includes a lobby and stairs leading down to the social area. Another staircase in the garden links the two levels. The main bedroom suite is situated on the upper floor with few walls, framing a panoramic view of the landscape, and sliding windows. The public space is on the lower floor and is accessed from the garden as well as from the upper-level entrance. A studio, living room, kitchen/dining area, terrace, garden and services are on this level. The emphasis placed on white surfaces, including the marble floors inside, gives the entire house a light, almost ethereal feeling.

The architects used a 'hybrid structure of concrete walls and steel … enabling a clean, ordered and efficient building site'. They state: 'The orientation and the exploitation of the natural terrain took a main role in the design process. It was meant to create functional spaces that maintained order and visual continuity, with a simple diagram of two horizontal crystal L forms and a vertical L form made of concrete.'

Pages 84–85 The crisply designed house has a broadly glazed lower floor facing a sheltered garden. On the upper balcony, a line of green plants contrasts with the dominant white forms.

Below A band of windows on the upper level gives a broad view of the environment in which the house is set.

Opposite The whiteness of the house is emphasized by bright lighting. The lower level goes without curtains because it is enclosed by garden walls.

Opposite The lower level glass walls slide open to create a sheltered yet open living area.

Above The lower level kitchen has surfaces that are in continuity with the wooden stairs. A degree of warmth is afforded by the use of this wood.

MATT

GIBSON

/

SHAKIN'

STEVENS

HOUSE

\

AUSTRALIA

This is a 200-square-metre (2,150 sq ft) addition to a Victorian worker's cottage set in Richmond near the Melbourne Cricket Ground. This popular area, located 3 kilometres (1.8 miles) from Melbourne's Central Business District, has been the object of gentrification in recent years but is still called 'gritty' by the architects. Behind the older structure, Matt Gibson created three extruded white cubes that were positioned 'to orchestrate views to green elements within the structure and to greenery within or beyond the site', because the client wanted a connection to green spaces. Thus symbolically, after white, green is the main colour of this project.

The three cubes appear not to touch, but materials continue through the volumes, effectively bringing the architecture and the interior design together. It was the client who requested a mainly white interior with a 'feature highlight colour'. The original house is painted in a light green with white accents, but has a bright green entrance door. Green was logically chosen for kitchen cabinets and the modular wall system in the living area. The project includes numerous 'green', or ecologically oriented, features as well, beginning with the orientation of the new addition, and including the use of recycled wood for flooring and of artificial grass to reduce water consumption, which is also alleviated by a grey-water recycling system. The unusual name of the house is related to the fondness of both the architect and the client for the singer Shakin' Stevens, who had a UK hit in 1981 with the song 'Green Door'.

Pages 90–91 The brightly coloured green door of the original house is related to the name of the house, inspired by a Shakin' Stevens song.

Opposite The rear, entirely new part of the house combines stacked white cubes with green interior surfaces and a wooden deck that extends outdoors.

Page 94 The stacked and open design offers a view from the upper level towards the ground-floor living space.

Page 95 The juncture between the old house and the new section is partially eased by the use of green-coloured surfaces, though white remains dominant.

Left An upper-floor view taken from the master bedroom, with a large opening framing the city.

Below The stairway connecting the ground and first floors reveals neighbouring rooftops.

Opposite The living area on the ground floor is enlivened by its panelled wall with shades ranging from dark green to yellow.

JAKOB

+

MACFARLANE

/

CONNECTED

HOUSE

\

FRANCE

This large 800-square-metre (8,600 sq ft) residence is located in the western suburbs of Paris, near the Molitor apartment block designed by Le Corbusier in 1931–34 at 24, rue Nungesser et Coli, where he lived and worked until his death in 1965. The architects state: 'The historical context of the house is important as a precedent for the project. It pursues the architectural tradition of experimental housing by architects in the 1920s and 1930s.' The house originally on the site was demolished, but its height and mass could not be exceeded for regulatory reasons. The owners decided to keep the late nineteenth-century chauffeur's cottage to the rear of the site as a guest house.

The Connected House bears a relation in terms of its conception to the natural structure of trees. The floors are supported by a branching, tubular steel structure and the architects have imagined the white, faceted aluminium skin of the house like tree bark. An exterior form consisting of irregular concentric rings was wrapped around a vertical circulation core. With four storeys above grade, the house also includes an underground lap pool. The name of the house is related to its connection to the city power grid, which it is intended to feed into using its own geothermal heating and energy.

Pages 98-99 The unusual house stands in a garden area, with paving stones that echo the forms of the panels used for cladding.

Below The first floor includes a large corner aquarium. Wood surfaces dominate, with white ceilings and columns.

Opposite A white-metal and wood staircase connects the different levels of the house (as does an elevator, not visible here).

J. MAYER H.

ARCHITECTS

/

DUPLI.CASA

\

GERMANY

The design of this 1,000-square-metre (10,760 sq ft) residence is based on a family house built on the same site in 1984 and subsequently extended and modified. According to the architect, the newer structure 'echoes the "family archaeology" by duplication and rotation'. The openings of the house offer views towards the old part of Marbach and the German Literature Archive, with its new wing designed by David Chipperfield (2006), located on the opposite side of the Neckar valley.

The three-storey house has its lower level partially inserted into the sloped site. The architect's diagrams show the careful attention that has gone into circulation patterns and the separation of public and private areas, with a semi-public space being generated at ground level where the house is lifted up. Almost entirely white, with black detailing for such features as the window frames, the residence is in some sense a study in contrasts – an organic-type volume dressed up in the colours of minimalism. The way that this unusual house appears to flow down its sloped site, with its forms sometimes cantilevered over the exterior terrace areas, makes the emphasis on movement and views quite clear. The architect says that the skin of the villa creates 'a sophisticated connection between inside and outside'.

Opposite The generous living space is augmented by double-height volumes and windows that provide overhead lighting.

Below, left The white surfaces flow and fold into the numerous sources of natural and artificial light.

Below, right Black floors and steps echo the black window and door areas. The forms of the house are unexpected and yet functional.

Pages 102–103 Despite its stark contrast between white forms and black window and door frames, the house has an almost organic presence, looking as though it might suddenly move.

Pages 104–105 A ground-floor pool is reflected in a mirror wall, giving an impression of very generous spaces bordered only by the nearby wall of greenery.

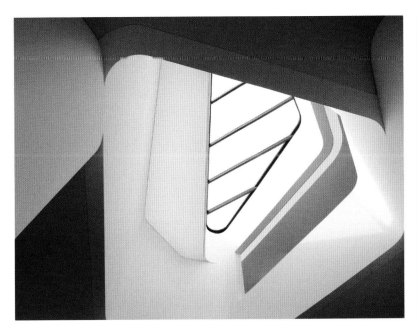

MCGONIGLE

MCGRATH

/

HOUSE

AT

MAGHERA

\

UK

Maghera is a village in County Down, just north of the small seaside resort of Newcastle. The house's forms are inspired by those of the *clachan* (small settlement or hamlet) on the edge of which it is located. The architects state: 'There is evidence within the settlement of a tradition relating to dwellings and their outbuildings, of simple pitched roof and gabled masonry forms, with roofs of slate or steel.' Starting with this inspiration, the architects sought to create a link between the new house and its setting. Two linear forms set at slightly different angles are joined at the roof. The folded appearance of the house makes it seem quite modern even though its shapes are derived from traditional and agricultural architecture.

The materials used for the house were chosen in reference to local farm structures. The walled entrance courtyard also underlines the relation of the design to local precedent. The walls 'frame a pedestrian stepped entrance connecting the house to the village, and the whole project sits on an embedded plinth which addresses adjoining ground levels', according to the architects. The house has black-painted timber windows and doors. The walls are covered in white render and the roof is finished with zinc. Inside, white is also dominant, with wooden floors and ample glazing.

Pages 108–109 The house projects an image of rarefied simplicity and a crispness imposed by straight lines and white volumes.

Left Although its white and grey volumes immediately project an image of modernity, the design also evokes more traditional local architecture.

Opposite The angled, abstract white and grey composition reveals little of interior volumes or function from this angle.

Opposite Wooden floors and cabinetry somewhat alleviate the otherwise strict black and white forms. Natural light comes from above in this view, as well as from generous ground-level glazing.

Above and right Detail views of the house show the considerable attention paid by the architects to details that contribute to an overall impression of coherence.

PEDONE

WORKING

/

VILLA

DI

GIOIA

\

ITALY

The Villa Di Gioia is located in the Apulia region of southern Italy and was designed as an example of sustainable architecture. The design makes use of recycled materials and puts an emphasis on passive strategies to reduce solar gain and increase natural ventilation. Photovoltaic cells on the roof, triple glazing, and an air-to-air heat pump add active elements to the ecological design. The gross floor area of the house is 872 square metres (9,386 sq ft).

The front of the house is clad in metal that envelopes a glass box containing the living areas. A tower-like form overlooks a central patio, which is the 'hub' of the residence. The living space with its glass walls overlooks a garden, while an open staircase leads to the sleeping area on the higher level. Though the materials used are typical of the region's architecture, the modern design 'pays tribute to the rationalist legacy'. The concrete frame of the house has external walls insulated with 10 centimetres (4 in.) of cork. Materials with high thermal mass were chosen to reduce energy usage. The wall coatings employed are made with 'natural hydraulic lime and fibre-reinforced siloxane-elastomer'. The living room on the western side is fully glazed, allowing heat conservation in winter, and its glass façades are shaded by mulberry trees in summer.

Pages 114–115 The open centre of the house is reached via a set of white suspended steps leading from the light-blue entry door.

Right An outdoor patio and some vegetation give a touch of life to the otherwise strict and linear composition. Large windows bring ample daylight into the residence.

Opposite Wooden stairs lead up from the ground floor, where white walls and furniture echo the overall whiteness of the structure.

Above Rectilinear and uniformly white, the house projects an image of efficiency and precision.

Right An opening emphasizes the close connection between the white house and its green natural environment.

ELEMENTAL FORMS

Is white a colour or rather the absence of colour? If white is formed by the combination of all other colours, it should logically be one itself, but this issue has long been debated. In symbolic terms white is often associated with purity, goodness and perfection. Pure white then: what could be simpler? And should not the architect who uses white walls be inspired by this analogy? White architecture could very well seek to be elemental, pure, simple and – why not? – geometric, Euclidean, primal in the sense of the absence of all complication. The houses published here are indeed reductive and mostly rectilinear. They may tend to demonstrate either that white itself is a result of a search for simplicity, or the reverse, that white imposes a rejection of complexity just as it sweeps aside all other shades. But this might be too simple; Richard Meier has long defended the idea that white best takes on the colours of its surroundings, from blue sky to setting sun, a colour apart and yet made of all other shades.

FRANCISCO

AIRES

MATEUS

ARQUITECTOS

/

HOUSE

IN

LEIRIA

\

PORTUGAL

Page 120 The Cala House (Madrid, Spain, 2015, Alberto Campo Baeza) is, like much of the architect's work, minimalist in its plan and design, privileging white surfaces and forms.

Pages 122-123 The very fundamental form of a house in this image, with no visible windows above ground, is echoed by a square lightwell.

This visually rather unusual 297-square-metre (3,200 sq ft) house looks out over Leiria, a town of about 125,000 people located in the central coastal region of Portugal. Entirely white, the residence appears to have the outline of a very ordinary house, but it is devoid of windows, and its volume is sharply cut out to create horizontal and vertical openings. The blank white forms of the house give it a decidedly abstract appearance, a modernity that belies the traditional form of the white volume. The lack of windows is explained by the architect's decision to close out the surrounding rather chaotic town environment.

Four bedrooms are located at street level, grouped around a central courtyard, forming a void at the base of the visible house. The slope in the site makes this space appear to be below grade. The living areas on the first floor are arrayed around the void at the centre of the house, which runs through three levels. The house's central opening is oriented towards the medieval castle of Leiria in the city centre to the west, and an outdoor deck made of granite also enjoys this view. The architects custom-designed furniture for the house.

Opposite The architects are among the most interesting in Portugal, challenging basic ideas about houses and larger buildings too.

Above In this house, even the planters are white, and the presence of a woman seems ethereal, like the house itself.

CADAVAL

&

SOLÀ-

MORALES

/

PM

HOUSE

\

MEXICO

A 280-square-metre (3,000 sq ft) residence located 50 kilometres (30 miles) south of Cancún, the PM House is set in lush vegetation. From the street, to the south, the house appears 'neutral', but inside the architects have sought to make it 'magical'. The centre of the structure is occupied by a sculptural staircase, rising from the living room. The living area opens towards a rear garden. Bedrooms oriented to sea views are located in the upper part of the house, and are intentionally simple.

The architects state: 'The south façade of the house is hard, closed and opaque, while the north façade is more permeable and ductile. The construction and finishes of the house seek to be as austere as possible ... In the end, it is the space, with its opening to the mangrove, to the sea, [to] the vegetation and to the white north light, that is the main protagonist of the house.' The house has a rectilinear plan and an equally rigorous, white profile.

Pages 126–127 Every element of the house – the pool, the white outside walls and the darker indentations – speaks of a reduction to fundamental forms.

Above Square openings in the wall do not reveal the function of interior spaces.

Opposite The same square openings are found at ground level, creating some liveliness in the walls that lead to the swimming pool.

Above A hammock hangs between
terrace walls, an invitation to
relax and contemplate the sky.

Opposite The clever use of levels
makes for an attractive overlapping
staircase structure, adding an
interesting sense of dimension
to the reception area.

ALBERTO

CAMPO

BAEZA

/

CALA

HOUSE

\

SPAIN

The strict white forms of the Cala House are typical of the minimalist work of Alberto Campo Baeza. But the external simplicity in fact conceals a more complex internal structure. Built on a sloped site, the Cala House offers generous views of the mountains west of Madrid and the urban landscape of the eastern part of the city. Because of the views, the architect placed the public areas of the house at the top.

A 12-metre-square (39 sq ft) grid plan was used, in part to respect the local building code. Within this framework, four smaller equal 6-metre (191/2-ft) squares were laid out. The internal design of the house is inspired by the *Raumplan* system pioneered by Adolf Loos, which provides in this instance for a spiral arrangement of double spaces that are turned through 90 degrees as they rise, creating a spatial richness not necessarily present in a strictly geometric plan. In 1930, Loos stated: 'My architecture is not conceived by drawings, but by spaces ... For me, the ground floor, first floor do not exist ... There are only interconnected continual spaces, rooms, halls, terraces ... Each space needs a different height ... These spaces are connected so that ascent and descent are not only unnoticeable, but at the same time functional.'[1]

Openings in the volume are calculated to bring in natural light. A combination of jasmine and vines was chosen for ground-level planting near the porches and also for the rooftop.

1. http://socks-studio.com/2014/03/03/i-do-not-draw-plans-facades-or-sections-adolf-loos-and-the-villa-muller/ accessed on 3 September 2018

Pages 132-133 Using a combination of high white walls, rectangular openings and a composition that could almost be called hieratic, Campo Baeza imposes his architecture in an otherwise 'normal' neighbourhood.

Opposite An outdoor terrace with a water basin offers limited views through a long narrow opening and gives an unfettered view of the sky.

Left, above and below Presented here empty of furnishings and objects, aside from the built-in bookshelves, the house expresses its white rigour inside as well as out.

Opposite A long rectangular pool sits in front of the house, offering a touch of colour in an otherwise largely monochromatic environment.

JIN

OTAGIRI

/

GHOST

HOUSE

\

JAPAN

The architect dared to call this 'one of the most minimalist houses in Japan'. Despite the modern, enigmatic appearance of the residence, he asserts too that he was seeking to recreate the 'archetypical primitive hut-like house'. Aside from the floors, the structure is entirely white, inside and out. The 'ghostly silhouette' seen outside is contrasted with 'eccentric' interior spaces that were the desire of the client. The project, located in Suginami ward, Tokyo, is in part an almost humorous response to the Japanese building code, which forbids many things but allows a totally blank house, as here.

Natural light is present inside but not through any visible windows. As is the case in many other entirely white houses, scale becomes difficult to determine here. The inside of the house is arranged on three levels connected by intricate ramps and steps.

Jin Otagiri was just twenty-eight years old when he designed this house. Edwin Heathcote in the *Financial Times* wrote in 2007: 'Sitting in a courtyard like an origami garden shed, the brilliant white, seemingly blind structure is a kind of stripped archetype, an idea of a house more than the real thing ... It could be Zen; it could be sensory deprivation. Either way it is an eerie and haunting building that develops a certain idea of "houseness" already explored by Swiss designers but handled here in a very Japanese manner.'

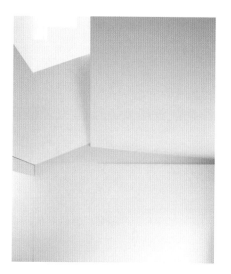

Pages 138–139 Possibly evoking a view of a beach, this picture actually shows nothing more than a close neighbouring wall.

Right, top to bottom Interiors benefit from natural light that comes from high openings, but they are otherwise very much in the white-on-white mode of the exterior.

Opposite The front façade of the house does have what looks like a door opening, but is otherwise totally blank.

JFGS

ARCHITECTS

/

GALLARDA

HOUSE

\

SPAIN

Pages 142–143 The more closed
upper volume of the house sits
on a broadly glazed, smaller
ground-floor volume.

Above The refined and distinct
elements of the exterior – glass,
concrete and stone – present a
strong contrast with the rough,
rocky site.

Right On the roof, which is
partially covered in gravel,
the white geometric forms of
the house draw a sharp line
across the rough landscape.

Built as a holiday residence by the sea for a 'young couple with an intense social life', the Gallarda House has a generous living and dining area, connected to the terraced outdoor space. The architect refers to the simple white houses in traditional Mediterranean architecture where 'man comes to happiness almost without realizing it'.

The floor area of the house is 215 square metres (2,315 sq ft), and it is built on a 1,200-square-metre (12,915 sq ft) site. The structure is divided into three superimposed parts, which the architect calls C1 (shaded and made of glass, near the pool and the garden); C2, a concrete volume inserted into the sloped site that 'belongs to the earth', and which the architect also calls the 'hole house'; and C3, made of 'lime, opacity and air, close to heaven, made to sleep and to dream'. C1 is in fact the middle volume placed between the other two sections of the residence. As the architect explains, the Gallarda House is heir to a tradition of whitewashed Mediterranean houses with windows that are protected from the sun and which are partially below grade.

JONAS

LINDVALL

/

VILLA

J2

\

SWEDEN

This project, located in a popular resort area in southern Sweden, began as an update to a 1940s summer house, but became a new build during the course of design because local regulations required that the footprint had to be left unchanged. The resulting forms are essentially linear and white. The rather closed entrance façade was designed to give the clients as much privacy as possible in their residential neighbourhood. A garage that is angled forward on the street side as compared to the main volume serves to isolate the residence, as do tall shrubs planted along the borders of the site.

Inside, a long, narrow hallway runs the full length of the house, leading to the master bedroom and two children's bedrooms. A playroom separates the children's space from the parents' area. A kitchen, dining and lounge area open to a west-facing patio, which is a central aspect of the plan. A white-painted steel spiral staircase with wooden steps under a skylight on the north side of the house leads up to a home office, library and terrace. The architect says that this 'dramatic, light-filled area was inspired by winter gardens of the past'.

Pages 146-147 A linear composition of white blocks with wooden doors, the house is both rigorous and enigmatic because of the apparent lack of windows.

Left Exterior façades open to simple terraces and a lawn. Here the glazing is relatively generous, making the interior spaces visible from the outside.

Below A spectacular winding spiral
staircase is bathed in light that
falls from above. A broad window
opens to the garden at ground level.

Above The bathroom, seen here
with its large curved tub and
stone washbasin, offers some
contrast to the strict white
lines of the volumes.

Opposite Natural wood panelling
adds warmth to the hallway, while
a floor-to-ceiling window invites the
outdoor environment into the house.

SHINICHI

OGAWA

/

LIBRARY

HOUSE

\

JAPAN

Pages 152-153 The streetside façade of the house is an enigmatic white composition with only a doorway visible. The walls of the building come directly down to a narrow, shallow trench that contains pebbles.

Above, left Despite the blankness of the house's exterior, inside, a wooden table, a bookshelf, and a long skylight give it both light and warmth.

Above, right A small courtyard to the rear of the house, just off the dining area, looks into a bathroom.

Built on a 315-square-metre (3,390 sq ft) site, this combined residence and office was constructed with reinforced concrete. The building footprint is 164 square metres (1,765 sq ft) and the total floor area of the one-storey structure is 156 square metres (1,680 sq ft). A white cubic volume contains the living and dining space with a 6-metre-high (20 ft) ceiling; a high bookshelf runs along the northern side. Natural light is admitted through a long, rectangular ceiling opening and also along the glazed southern elevation, which faces a courtyard. The light is modulated using an exterior awning.

There are no corridors and all the other spaces of the house can be accessed directly from the central volume. The larger courtyard in the design faces the living and dining areas as well as the master bedroom and the office. A smaller courtyard faces the living and dining spaces as well as a child's room and the bathroom.

Seen from the outside, the interior of the house is difficult to discern – the exterior is characterized by blank white walls. Inside, white is also the rule, contributing to an overall impression of colourless purity, interrupted only by the wall of books.

PAULÍNY

HOVORKA

ARCHITEKTI

/

DOM

ZLOMU

\

SLOVAKIA

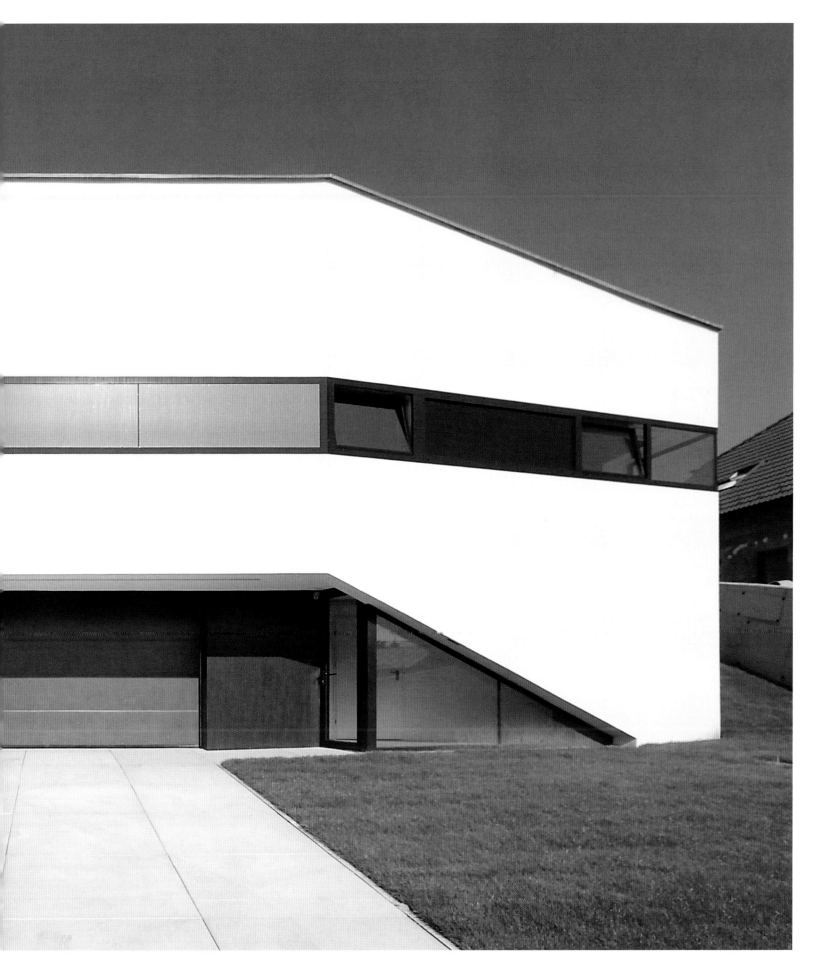

Located in Kynceľová, a small village close to Banská Bystrica in central Slovakia, Dom Zlomu was built for a client who requested a single-storey structure with a maximum amount of daylight. The 239-square-metre (2,570 sq ft) house was built on a 1,100-square-metre (11,840 sq ft) eastward-sloping site and ended up with its entrance on a lower level, but the rest of the programme is on a single level with full-height glazing wherever possible.

The spaces are divided into day areas parallel to the street, including living room, kitchen and home office; and night areas, with the master bedroom and two bedrooms for children facing a rear garden. The main level of the house is cantilevered in the direction of the street in order to shelter the entrance. The architects explain: 'This way, the mass and the visual impact of the street façade is also reduced. This is further supported by means of colouring the basement black contrasting with the white render of the rest of the house.'

The architects were also responsible for interior design and landscaping for this house. High-gloss white furnishings were chosen in order to 'organically blend with the building fabric'. The structure of the house is in reinforced concrete with infill brick masonry. The flat roof is covered with a PVC membrane.

Pages 156-157 The rather powerful white form of the house appears to be lifted off the ground to make way for a garage. A long slit window winds from the front façade to the side.

Opposite, above The house sits close to a neighbouring structure, whose yellow garage seems chosen to oppose the black and white sparseness of Dom Zlomu.

Opposite, below The custom-designed kitchen might almost seem to be a scale model of the house itself, with the upward slant of the purely white work surface.

TAKURO

YAMAMOTO

/

WHITE

CAVE

HOUSE

\

JAPAN

The White Cave House is entirely white, in part as an echo of the typical snowfalls in Kanazawa, and has a floor area of 172 square metres (1,850 sq ft). The architect has conceived of it as a series of voids, within the typology of the Japanese courtyard house but somehow different as well. The client wanted a white, minimal house with numerous outdoor spaces, including an entrance protected from the typically heavy snow of this region.

The architect explains the thinking behind the concept of the house: 'We proposed to connect the external spaces one to the other in a large single tube, or Cave, and have each part serve multiple purposes in order to make up for the space limitations. We designed the Cave to be *unstraight* because it prevents those outside from seeing in, though it is not closed. With this arrangement, the Cave takes a new turn for each part, letting in the sun while protecting the privacy of the courtyard, the terrace, and the internal rooms. The family inside can enjoy the view of the Cave's changing light throughout a day.' Addressing the difficulty of clearing snow from an enclosed courtyard, the Cave also serves as 'a route to remove snow from external spaces in winter...'. A terrace covered in white waterproof FRP (fibre-reinforced plastic) retains a thin layer of water, forming a white basin.

The strict, often closed volumes as seen from the outside in all of their whiteness, echoed by the use of white inside, make this into a luminous space where dimensions and time can seem to dissolve.

Pages 160-161 The design of the house seems to focus mainly on geometric simplicity and an absence of many of the usual points of recognition for a house, such as visible windows in this instance.

Opposite The unexpected entry provides ample protection from heavy snowfalls. The driveway and the grass surroundings of the house are nearly as minimalist as the building itself.

Left The external spaces of
the house are interconnected by
what the architect calls a 'large
single tube'. Single trees stand
out from the otherwise entirely
white environment.

Right A dark ledge or bench
extends in an unexpected way
from the interior living space
into a courtyard area.

Above Whiteness creates an almost
seamless link between the exterior
courtyard and the interior kitchen/
dining space.

TSUKANO

ARCHITECT

OFFICE

/

HOUSE

T

\

JAPAN

This small house is located in the downtown area of Miyazaki, a city on the island of Kyushu in the south of Japan. The site borders a busy road, with tall residential buildings to the south. The architect, who attributes 'a brilliant idea' to himself, says that his solution consists in creating a 'white wrap' around the home, which sets it aside from the crowded environment while allowing natural light to be admitted via an internal courtyard.

The reinforced-concrete structure was built on a 172-square-metre (1,850 sq ft) site and has a total floor area of 108 square metres (1,163 sq ft) over two storeys. Within the essentially square plan, there is a dining area, kitchen, study and courtyard on the ground floor, and a bedroom and living area on the upper level. In section the house is also strictly rectilinear. House T is as close as one might care to come to a simple, closed, white box, with hardly any opening visible to outsiders. The idea of bringing in natural light from above, in this instance through a courtyard, has been used frequently in crowded Japanese cities but, in this case, it is the blank whiteness of the house that stands out in a quite radical fashion.

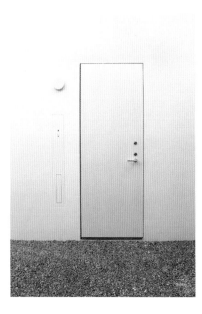

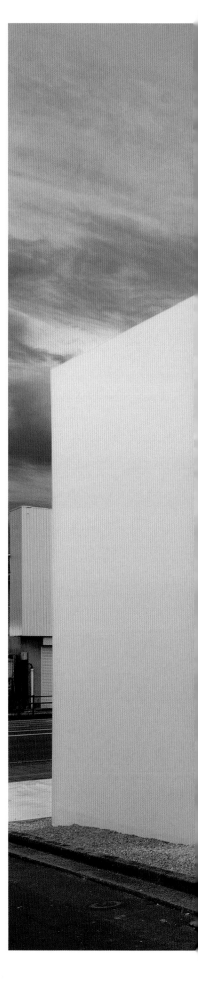

Pages 166–167 The exterior of the house offers few clues as to the interior disposition of its spaces.

Page 170 Inside the house, wooden surfaces give some relief from the spotless whiteness of the exterior.

Left and right The rear of the house hardly varies from the otherwise blank whiteness of the volume.

Page 171 The kitchen and a connected dining space are at the heart of the first-floor plan, enjoying diffuse natural light.

URBAN OASES

Walls that are white, perhaps more than those in other shades, seem to mark a limit between a chaotic exterior world and a protected inside. A white house may speak of order and a clear division between what is private and what is public. White 'order' is opposed to the multicoloured disorder of the uncurated world outside the walls. Inside geometric white barriers, the private life of a house owner and his or her guests is clearly set apart from outside interference or disorder. Design makes the world new in some sense, offering protection, creating what might be called an urban oasis in the case of the houses published here. Interior worlds develop and evolve within the confines of modern whiteness. An alternative is to create a white inner sanctum within a fenced garden, as De Matos Ryan do in their London Garden House (page 174). Whatever the defensive posture of an urban residence towards its environment, white is likely to set any house apart, to distance it from any neighbours, even the closest ones.

DE

MATOS

RYAN

/

GARDEN

HOUSE

\

UK

The Garden House is a 179-square-metre (1,930 sq ft) residence built in the garden behind a Victorian house in the Battersea area of southwest London. The new house was needed for a recomposed family with seven children. The arrival of an eighth child prompted the parents to move into the newer five-bedroom structure with their baby and younger children, leaving the original house to the older children.

A bridge leads to the new house, bisecting its white-block volume. The architects undertook mandatory flood protection work owing to the proximity of the house to the river Thames. Fully glazed living areas are located at the level of an excavated white concrete courtyard, with bedrooms above. The bedrooms receive natural light from lightwells and rooflights. The architects state: 'A playful improbability of form manifests itself throughout the scheme: from a floating dining table cantilevered from the kitchen worktop to the apparent mass of the upper volumes that appear to float above a glass wall. This playfulness was a key aspiration for the project to add to the surprise and delight of discovering a house at the bottom of a garden.'

Page 172 The Covert House by DSDHA is hidden from view in a conservation area in Clapham Old Town, London.

Pages 174–175 The site of the house is protected by a fence formed with vertical wooden slats, meaning that its white and grey volume is amply protected from the street.

Opposite The blank white upper volume of the house sits on a completely glazed ground level, which has been excavated to protect the space walls, while allowing light to penetrate fully.

Above The glass walls of the ground level can be withdrawn, creating a living space that is at once covered and outdoors.

Opposite Steps lead down to the enclosed terrace space around the house.

Below The interior staircase leads up to the five bedrooms housed in the 'floating' white volume that is most visible from the outside.

Left The kitchen, with its wooden surfaces, cantilevered white table and touches of grey, opens to the exterior terrace space and has ample natural light.

DSDHA

/

COVERT

HOUSE

\

UK

The Covert House is located in a conservation area of Clapham Old Town in London. Designed and built by DSDHA directors Deborah Saunt and David Hills for their own use, this 135-square-metre (1,450 sq ft) house was built with a modest budget. Seeking to disturb the site – formerly an overgrown space between two rear gardens – as little as possible, the architects set this house partially into the ground to meet local height restrictions. Sunken courtyards provide natural light for every room. The architects state: 'Within its resolutely sculpted form, the building carefully uses openness and light to transition between inside and outside as well as to connect the upper and lower floors.'

It is an in-situ concrete structure with open-plan living spaces that include a double-height living area containing a white concrete staircase. Ample glazing and white surfaces make the structure seem to be extremely light, standing out against its green setting near mature trees. The house has a green roof and triple-glazed windows. The concrete used for the structure takes advantage of thermal mass to reduce heat loss (or gain). An air source heat pump and radiant heating through the resin floors are used, as well as rainwater harvesting for toilets and garden irrigation. The Covert House received a RIBA London Award (2016) and was a RIBA House of the Year Award finalist (2016).

Pages 182–183 A light, glazed pavilion emerges above grade, with a hint of the larger volume below visible in the foreground.

Opposite A narrow lily pond and a planter step down towards a courtyard in front of the lower-level part of the structure.

Page 186 The concrete walls and ceiling contrast with the white simplicity of the floor and kitchen cabinets.

Page 187 A light staircase winds up to the ground level. Except for the grey walls, white is the rule here, including for the window frames.

Left Furnishing is summary, allowing the white and grey surfaces to define the indoor spaces.

Opposite The minimal atmosphere of the interiors is accented by a lack of all but the essential elements of day-to-day life.

JMY

ARCHITECTS

/

172M2

COMPACT

HOUSE

\

SOUTH

KOREA

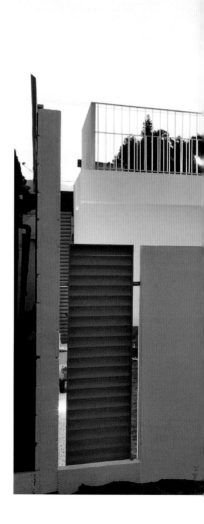

GYEONGJU, SOUTH KOREA, 2014

This residence was built on a south-facing rectangular 172-square-metre (1,850 sq ft) lot in a fairly dense suburban zone in the city of Gyeongju in southeastern South Korea. The architect points out that in this residential suburb, that area is 'just enough to have a house with three rooms and a small garden'. The goal was to create a space that is secluded from the outside, but open inside, with a living space that is transparent from the south-side garden to the northern backyard. The design also allows for division of the existing space into smaller rooms as required. The outer walls have no windows, to preserve the privacy of the owners, but slits and skylights bring in ample natural light. Ventilation windows are placed on each side to allow for natural air circulation, no matter what the direction of the winds.

The house has an 88-square-metre (947 sq ft) footprint and a total floor area of 134 square metres (1,440 sq ft). The two-storey reinforced-concrete building has a silicon paint finish on the exterior and acrylic paint inside. The entirely white exterior of the house makes it stand out in its architecturally heterogeneous environment. Wooden outdoor decks, interior floors and some walls add a touch of warmth to the house, which otherwise offers a rather closed or cold appearance from the exterior.

Pages 190-191 The house contrasts with its neighbourhood, not so much because of the roof terrace but because of its distinctive white colouring.

Right Perimeter walls and lighting make the house stand out in its strict, rectilinear whiteness.

Below The combined living, dining
and kitchen area is large and open,
with wooden furniture and floors
warming the otherwise bare, white,
glazed space.

Opposite The crisp upper-storey
guardrail seems to be carved
directly out of the white
substance of the house.

JVA

/

POLITE

HOUSE

\

NORWAY

A single-family residence located in a residential area of the city of Trondheim called Havstein, the Polite House has a floor area of 170 square metres (1,830 sq ft). The project involved a number of constraints, including 'a neighbourhood with varied density and architectural expressions', and an imposed distance between the house and the adjoining road. The narrow site inspired the architects to go towards a 'strong verticality'. The vertical form allows the living room to have views across the city to the fjord to the north, while a terrace provides an outdoor space on the south side. The compact plan combines functions, allowing the kitchen and dining room to come together, making a hallway into a play area, or, more unexpected, blending the office area with guest space.

The architects state: 'The vase-like expression of the house has emerged from minimal details, along with an exterior and interior cladding in white fibre cement panels. Ceilings are in birch plywood and the floor is made in epoxy terrazzo cast on site that gives a warm atmosphere to the interior.'

Pages 196-197 The house appears to be made up of three stacked and slightly skewed volumes, with touches of colour inside contrasting with the white walls.

Opposite A black hanging fireplace, modern furnishings and light fixtures bring the living and dining spaces to life.

Above An angled window in the bathroom immediately gives a modern feeling to the space.

Right The exterior of the house has a number of unexpected angles; here, the roof overhangs a small terrace on the first floor.

Above A suspended rotating fireplace
(Bathyscafocus) hangs between the
kitchen and living areas.

OHLAB

/

MM

HOUSE

\

SPAIN

The MM House, made up of four connected box-like forms, is located on a sloped 2,000-square-metre (21,530 sq ft) site near Palma on the Balearic island of Mallorca. The angled structure was built with reinforced concrete and has an exterior insulation system and a white stucco finish. The different angles of the building are intended to adapt to the site and to differing views. Each of the boxes that make up the 195-square-metre (2,100 sq ft) house has a different function, but all have large glazed surfaces contrasting with their otherwise white simplicity.

The central volume at the entrance has a living and dining space and a rooftop balcony. The kitchen occupies another volume, while the bedrooms are located in the remaining two boxes. Furniture and window frames are in pine, while beige and green tiles are used for the floors throughout. Radiant floor heating and cooling (using chilled water) are employed according to the season. Ecological concerns are addressed with passive means such as natural ventilation and windows angled to avoid the summer sun, and with active systems such as a solar water heater and a heat pump. Rainwater is collected and used for irrigation, and with appropriate filtering for drinking water as well, making the house, at least in theory, autonomous in terms of water.

Pages 202–203 Angled surfaces and volumes and touches of colour enliven the otherwise entirely white house.

Left An upper terrace and the ground level are visible with their green, white and tan tile floors.

Opposite Natural stone walls follow the movement of the white house down the slope of the site.

Opposite This bedroom features
a panoramic window and a sliding
wooden door that reveals the
adjoining bathroom.

Above, left The bathroom has wall
and floor tiling that resembles
that used elsewhere in the house.

Above, right The same tile pattern
is used on the living-room floor.
A very light, white staircase leads
up to the private spaces.

PARASITE

STUDIO

/

C

HOUSE

\

ROMANIA

Located in a recently built suburb of Timisoara, in the west of Romania, this 530-square-metre (5,700 sq ft) house is composed essentially of white volumes with black accents. The architects explain: 'The white colour highlights the volume's horizontal/vertical dynamics, and the black colour has the role of visually stretching and emphasizing the openings.'

The main façade of the house engages a street and faces east. The southern elevation is designed to bring as much daylight into the house as possible. A backyard with a swimming pool and a large green lawn is located near the more transparent western façade; and finally, on the western side, the design favours a certain opacity.

The living area is the pivotal point of the design, where horizontal and vertical circulation is concentrated. The floating white staircase here is designed to encourage natural airflow through the house. The master bedroom and children's rooms are located on the upper level. Inside, the wilful contrast between white and black is a recurring theme from the kitchen to the chimney.

Pages 208-209 The angled white volumes of the house are starkly contrasted with the black finishing around all of the openings. A light black line also marks the horizontal demarcation of each level.

Opposite The entrance contrasts black and white, adding a line of white stones and a sculptural dwarf pine to the sequence.

Above To the rear, the house lifts up and offers each floor access to outdoor spaces and covered exterior areas.

Above The bathroom seen here is a study in material contrasts in grey, white and tan.

Opposite Furnishings such as the coffee table echo the forms of the house. Although white is the rule, warm wooden floors and black surfaces again provide strong contrasts.

PITSOU

KEDEM

/

J

HOUSE

\

ISRAEL

The large 800-square-metre (8,610 sq ft) J House, located in the affluent coastal city of Hertzliya in the district of Tel Aviv, has a dramatic broad inverted and asymmetric V roof and generous bright spaces. The openings in the house, including frequent instances of full-height glazing and a long white metal lattice structure, bring filtered daylight directly inside in a constantly changing way.

Reflecting pools and an entrance bridge contribute to a sense of movement, while a large outdoor canopy extends from the house to cover the lounge area near the pool. Inside, wooden floors provide a note of warmth to the otherwise white or white-and-grey marbled environment, with black accents. The design makes way for strong contrasts between opacity and transparency and also in terms of colour and lighting, as can be seen in the dark bar and living area. Two floors are reserved for the bedrooms, 'intersected by common split-levels', in the three-storey structure.

The house is set within a walled garden that contributes to a sense of protection in the otherwise very open architectural composition. The plan is a careful orchestration of rectilinear forms with diagonals appearing prominently in section. Although the house's white forms speak in the first instance of a Modernist bias, the complexity and interplay not only of the basic architectural forms but also of largely decorative elements like the lattice screens place the design in a decidedly contemporary mode.

Pages 214–215 The angled roof, approach bridge and openwork grille that crosses almost the entire façade, make the appearance of this white house unique.

Opposite In this view of a stairway, steel wires contrast with a rough wall. Light and forms create a striking, abstract composition.

Left, top to bottom Stairways, water and sunlight come together to create unusual shadows and reflections.

Below The living room area is fully glazed and can be almost entirely opened to the terrace and garden.

Opposite Hanging black light fixtures above the kitchen area continue the overall theme of strong and unexpected contrasts and combinations of colour and form.

ABRAHAM

COTA

PAREDES

ARQUITECTOS

/

THE

CAVE

\

MEXICO

This 390-square-metre (4,200 sq ft) house is located in the metropolitan area of Guadalajara, where perimeter walls are typical for security reasons. This fact inspired the architect to contemplate 'the search for isolation and shelter, for what generates introspective architecture'. Privacy, the fluidity of spaces and the management of light were three of the design priorities for this residence.

A multipurpose family room is located in the level of the house that is below grade. A double-height internal patio with a tree brings natural light and ventilation to this basement space. Facing the back of the plot, the dining room is also a double-height space. Rooms for children are located on the second level.

The architect describes the exterior form of the house as a 'cube that sits on a stone base, seeking to be as closed as possible', yet providing the openings 'necessary to provoke in the viewer an interest in knowing what goes on inside'. The play on whiteness and ample, rather surprising spaces inside the house gives this 'cave' a light-filled aspect that might seem to contradict its name. The Cave instead is a kind of private enclosed world, safe from the outside and yet somehow open within.

Pages 220-221 Although built in a rather densely packed residential neighbourhood, the house stands out because of its crisp white lines and relative blankness.

Opposite Stone steps, a wooden door and abstract openings immediately differentiate the house from the next-door structure.

Above An entirely linear and white volume finds welcome contrast in a variegated timber floor.

Right In an unexpected configuration, marble steps emerge from an angled, white enclosure.

Opposite Outdoor walls and floors are clad in rough, irregular stone.

ATELIER

TEKUTO

/

REFLECTION

OF

MINERAL

\

JAPAN

Set on a tiny 44-square-metre (474 sq ft) lot, this reinforced-concrete structure has a footprint of just 31 square metres (334 sq ft). The three-storey house has a basement and a total floor area of 86 square metres (926 sq ft). The architect states: 'The client had three requests; for their home to be a highly stimulating piece of architecture, to achieve maximum liveable volume; to have a covered parking space for their car.'

The complex form of the house was the result of the architect's need to take local building codes into account in achieving the programme requested by the client. The only symmetrical form in the plan is the rectangular parking spot, and even here, the walls are angled. As the corner plot itself has an irregular pentagonal form, the resulting composition is compared by the architect to 'a piece of mineral that is buried in the ground'.

The interior of the house has an almost Piranesian complexity, with various open and mezzanine spaces that intersect at unexpected angles. These forms also bring in natural light in changing ways, filtering from the large windows through the internal intricacy of the space. The architect says: 'The process of deciding on the final form was like giving cuts to a precious gemstone – we worked with the utmost precision to do this and the result was like a shining piece of diamond.' That said, diamonds are generally cut in symmetrical forms, and that is not the case here. The whiteness of the house certainly has a relation to the mineral references of the architects.

Pages 226-227 In a typical dense Tokyo residential area, the house stands out not only because it is entirely white, but because of its angles and unusual, single large window.

Opposite The layering of the levels of the house and the unusual form of the openings extends to the kitchen space, which offers glimpses of the upper area.

Left, top to bottom Interior views show the continuity of the angled architecture and also the active play on natural and artificial light.

YAZGAN

DESIGN

/

WHITE

HOUSE

\

TURKEY

An 800-square-metre (8,610 sq ft) four-storey residence, the White House was designed for a large family. The programmatic elements of the house, including the entrance, foyer, living room, kitchen, dining room, master bedroom, study, children's rooms, storage room, fitness room and garage, were conceived as distinct elements arranged around a central focal point. A staircase and an elevator in the central core allow movement between the levels. This core, together with the perimeter walls, provides the structural support required, allowing interior spaces to be quite open. Each of the rooms receives natural light from two directions, from the exterior and from the centre.

The exterior design is in good part a result of the interior requirements of the client, creating what the architect calls a 'sense of push and pull', with a dynamic relationship between inside and outside. The outside of the house is painted white; reflective materials were used at the terrace level and on extensions, which include a greenhouse. As well as the large terrace on the top floor, there is a wooden veranda area at ground level.

The plan shows an irregular four-armed design with rounded corners. High glazed walls bring ample natural light into the living areas of this house, which stands out from neighbouring residences thanks to both its whiteness and its unusual forms.

Pages 230-231 Although the house is located close to neighbouring properties, it has a distinctive monumentality, expressed in both its curved forms and its ample glazing.

Opposite Horizontal bands characterize the exterior surfaces, where on occasion a black form interrupts the overall whiteness.

WATERSIDE

REFLECTIONS

It would seem that white houses thrive on contrast. Be it against the colours of the sky, or, perhaps better still, the blue expanse of the sea, modern white forms take on life and stand out even more when they are in the presence of water. Even a swimming pool provides a shift in perception, from planar opacity to light-blue depth. By definition, water is the opposite of the relative aridity of white architectural forms, bringing a different kind of movement with a breeze and a splash. The ultimate presence of water, though, is in the endless expanse of the sea, making it seem that a white house is a kind of frame, or a viewing platform for gazing at the infinite. Some, but of course not all, white houses near the sea are very much an effort to abolish limits, to make white geometric abstraction merge with the endless horizon. Sometimes, the expanse of the sea is contrasted not only with white architecture, but also with a rocky coast. Whiteness might be seen as a rejection of ever-changing nature, or perhaps as an ordered place to take in and absorb mutability.

314

ARCHITECTURE

STUDIO

/

H3

HOUSE

\

GREECE

The H3 House was built in the eastern suburbs of Athens on a 7,000-square-metre (74,350 sq ft) plot. The total floor area of the residence is 1,000 square metres (10,750 sq ft). The architect explains: 'The design objective was to create a luxurious and ergonomic environment with clean lines and minimalist aesthetic.' The design of the house also takes into account environmental concerns, with a geothermal system for cooling and heating and photovoltaic panels to the rear of the plot that provide electricity.

White is, of course, typical of Greek houses, and in this instance the image of 'clean lines' is highlighted by the unified colouring (or lack of colouring). The entire house and its furnishings, also worked on by the architect, create an aerodynamic or 'ergonomic' feeling that might once have been called 'futuristic'. Although the two main support columns beneath the otherwise cantilevered main volume are angled, as is the rear of the house, most other forms employed are strictly rectilinear. The client is fond of yachting, one reason that artificial ponds, fed from a well, were created around the house; the pools also give a cooling sensation in the warm Greek climate. Wall pieces by the sculptor John Aspras were part of the overall project. The H3 House was nominated for the 2015 Mies van der Rohe European Union Prize.

Page 234 An aqua pool cedes to the dark blue of the Sea of Crete in the Summer House (Santorini, Greece, 2017, Kapsimalis Architects).

Pages 236-237 Angled columns give the suspended house a sense of movement despite its rather blank volume as seen from this angle.

Pages 238-239 The house and the large protective covering over the outdoor seating area seem to hover above the pool. Black surfaces contrast with the overall whiteness of the house.

Left The forms and volumes of the house have a markedly abstract character, while the pool surrounds a good part of the living space.

Above In the master bedroom a black outdoor screen on the windows affords the only substantive contrast to the otherwise white environment.

Opposite In the living room, there is almost no relief from the three-dimensional whiteness that responds to and complements the exterior of the residence.

DWEK

ARCHITECTURE

+

PARTNERS

/

SILVER

HOUSE

\

GREECE

Cephalonia is the largest of the Ionian Islands, in the west of Greece. The architect says that when he was offered the opportunity to build on the island of Zakynthos, facing Cephalonia's coastline and its highest mountain peak, it was obvious to him that 'The subject would of course be the island [of Cephalonia], framed by the house. From the initial sketches until its completion, the plans were developed around the view. From the terraces, the sitting room, the dining room, kitchen, bedrooms and bathrooms, the living space was oriented towards this fascinating seascape, which the architecture emphasizes, making it even more theatrical.'

Given Greece's sunny climate, it was an obvious idea to make interior and exterior communicate extensively. Large sliding doors in the living and dining areas open to patios. The use of white echoes local architecture, surely inspired by the contrasting blue of the sea and the intense sunlight. The architect also took inspiration from the work of the French artist Yves Klein (1928–62), who said, 'Blue has no dimensions, it is beyond dimensions'. Olivier Dwek clearly sees the blue of Klein in the Mediterranean site of this house.

Interiors are set out in a minimalist fashion, with white again dominant, albeit with black details such as the window frames.

Pages 244-245 An outdoor terrace culminating in an infinity pool frames a remarkable view of Cephalonia and the broad blue expanse of the Ionian Sea.

Left At the rear of the house the rough stones of the site give way to the white geometric composition of the house, with concrete and tan gravel providing the transition.

Pages 248–249 The kitchen space
offers the same kind of bold forms
as the rest of the house, while
black counter tops and window
frames stand in stark contrast
to the mainly white surfaces.

Left Glazed walls with black frames
can be withdrawn to open large parts
of the house to the exterior.

Left, below The house sits in
pristine isolation on a sloped,
forested site overlooking the
Ionian Sea.

Opposite An open corner allows
residents to step directly onto the
outside terraces. Inside, a work by
Jean-Michel Basquiat brings colour
to the home.

KAPSIMALIS

ARCHITECTS

/

SUMMER

HOUSE

\

GREECE

Located in a traditional village, this cave-like house has a small exterior volume above grade. A living room and a small kitchen, as well as two bedrooms, a hammam and a sauna, are in the lower part of the house, which is built into the volcanic rock of the island. An infinity pool and a partially open vaulted space outside used for dining and lounging offer a platform with views of the Aegean Sea. The existing 'cave house' has amorphous curves that have formed the 'sculptural living space', while the small pool was imagined as quite literally hanging from the cliff edge. The opposition between the shadows inside and the bright sun outside are clearly part of the scheme as well.

The architects used gunite (concrete applied with a high-pressure hose) for the reconstruction of the house and the exterior supports, while volcanic stones and white plaster were employed for the interior and exterior walls. Light beige Vratza marble was used for the floors of the house, which has an interior area of about 100 square metres (1,075 sq ft), and cement plaster (Novamix) covers the walls and floors of the bathroom, sauna and hammam. Window frames are in niangon, an African tropical wood.

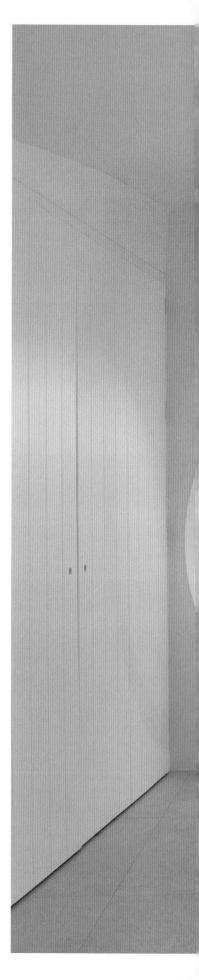

Pages 252–253 An aerial view of the house shows the swimming pool and deck area with a stretched canvas cover over the outdoor living space.

Right A pivoting glass opening leads from a hallway to a bedroom. White surfaces reflect and diffuse natural light.

Pages 256–257 The living room with rounded volumes and built-in counter or couch surfaces opens to the pool and a broad view of the Aegean Sea.

Below The rounded volumes, relatively simple furniture, rug and plants lend warmth to the ambient whiteness of the house.

Above Under the canopy, near the pool, the white shapes of the house are a canvas for crisply defined shadows.

Opposite Lounge chairs near the small pools are surrounded by white walls that direct views to the blue sea below.

MÁRIO

MARTINS

ATELIER

/

CASA

ELÍPTICA

\

PORTUGAL

LUZ, LAGOS, PORTUGAL, 2014

Luz, known for its beaches, is located on the southern Atlantic coast of Portugal, 6 kilometres (3.7 miles) from the town of Lagos. The Casa Elíptica, a 400-square-metre (4,300 sq ft) residence, readily assumes the intense white surfaces that are typical of this region. According to the architect, 'A balance was sought between fullness and emptiness, weight and airiness, light and shade, or the object and its image. It is a relationship between the real and the imagined, between physical and virtual spaces.'

The concrete house has an elliptical base and a very large cantilevered open ellipse that hovers above the central patio, a form that is imagined to have been carved out of the landscape by the wind. Most of the public spaces of the house are on the ground floor, including the patio. The house has open views of the ocean but is located close to another residence to the east, with which Mário Martins has sought to create a 'subtle connection'. Although the design is fluid and organic, the white forms of the house and its interior also announce a minimalist intention.

Pages 260-261 The cantilevered open ellipse of the house shades terrace areas and invites residents to feel a connection between the sky and the sea.

Right An aerial view reveals a kind of implied spiral in the plan leading from the broadest end of the pool to the interior of the house.

Opposite In many closer views, the house appears to approach complete abstraction, here alternating white and black, water and planar surfaces.

Right, above The suspended ellipse is undoubtedly the most unusual feature of the house. It gives only partial shade, but as the sun moves so do the shadows it casts.

Right The architect makes intelligent use of light and form. Here the white walls are crisply defined against the blue sky.

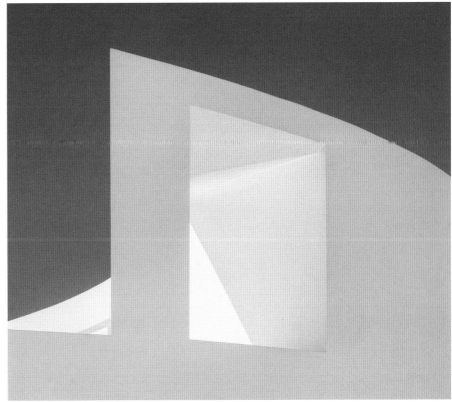

FRAN

SILVESTRE

ARQUITECTOS

/

CLIFF

HOUSE

\

SPAIN

As its name implies, this house was built on a steep cliff, looking down on the Mediterranean. Seeking to reduce complex excavation work on this site, the architect chose to use reinforced-concrete screens and slabs anchored in the rock for the one-storey structure. Partially inserted into the slope at the rear, the house cantilevers out in the direction of the sea. A swimming pool is located below, where the slope is less pronounced. The concrete has a layer of exterior insulation, and the house is covered in white lime stucco.

The architect has consistently shown a preference for the use of white in his houses, confirmed here by the material choices for the roof gravel and pavement. The white perfection of the house forms a wilful contrast with the rock setting above the blue sea. The plans of the house are made up of a strict composition of rectangles, with no curves anywhere. The interior design is the work of Alfaro Hofmann. Built for a cost of 650,000 euros, the house has a floor area of 242 square metres (2,605 sq ft). The architect states: 'We like the virtue of architecture that makes it possible to construct a house on the air, walking on water ... An abrupt plot of land overlooking the sea, where what is best is to do nothing. It is an invitation to stay.'

Opposite, above The linearity of the house and pool contrasts with the sloping outcrop, but somehow echoes the line of the horizon.

Opposite, below left This outdoor terrace is cut into the rocky site, imposing white, geometric order on the irregularities of nature.

Opposite, below right The perpendicular volumes of the house form an abstract composition.

Pages 266-267 Reflecting the rocky Costa Brava and looking out to sea, the house seems like a refuge of perfection in its craggy site.

Above With its long, rectangular opening suspended above the slope, the house defines itself in contrast with the environment in which it is immersed.

Right The living and dining space is defined with the same kind of white geometry as the house itself. Floor-to-ceiling glazing privileges the view.

Opposite A narrow staircase interrupts an otherwise pristine white wall. The living space is suspended as though to better take in the vast views of the sea.

Below At night, the house alternates between openness and opacity, light and dark, with just a suggestion of the roughness of nature.

Above A bathroom window looks
directly out onto the rocks of the
site, providing a complete contrast
to the smooth white surfaces inside.

TONKIN

LIU

/

NESS

POINT

\

UK

Located near the White Cliffs of Dover at Ness Point, with a broad view of the English Channel 65 metres (213 ft) below, the Ness Point house has a floor area of 439 square metres (4,725 sq ft). Set into the site with undulating walls, the residence is designed to take in the views, including the sun rising and setting over the water. The architects liken the protective design to a castle, but one that 'utilizes modern heat recovery and solar thermal renewable systems to maximize energy efficiency in the winter, whilst the long gallery skylight enables controlled passive cooling in the summer'. It also uses such energy-saving strategies as a green roof.

Despite its large size, the house was built on a strict budget. It has a curving or undulating form corresponding to the location, which allows the careful insertion of the structure into its windy, rather rugged site. Full-height glazing brings in the views. Inclined sections combine with this plan to generate 'cavernous internal space that allows flexibility of use'. White is the colour of predilection for this house, both inside and out. Though white contrasts with the immediate environment, it echoes the nearby White Cliffs.

Pages 274–275 The undulating lines of the house offer slightly different angles of view through each of the large windows.

Opposite, above An upper-floor balcony offers a view to the ground floor as light streams in from above, reflected and accentuated by the white surfaces.

Opposite, below A curved window looks out across the English Channel from a vantage point near the White Cliffs of Dover.

PLANS

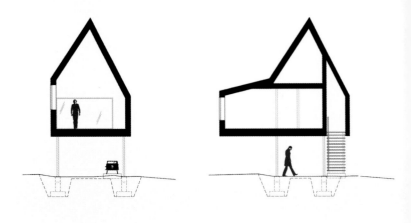

DELORDINAIRE
HIGH HOUSE_page 016

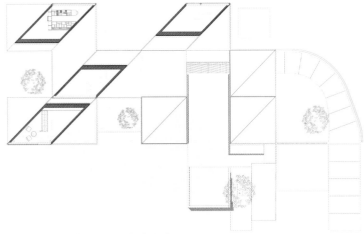

OAB – CARLOS FERRATER PARTNERSHIP
AA HOUSE_page 020

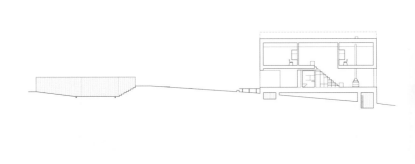

JOÃO MENDES RIBEIRO
FONTE BOA HOUSE_page 028

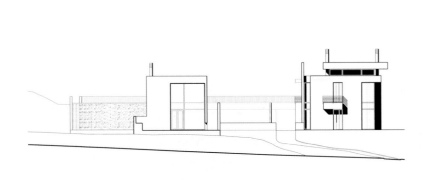

RICHARD MEIER
OXFORDSHIRE RESIDENCE_page 034

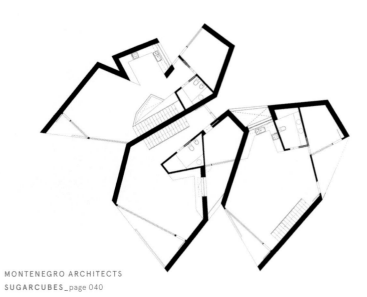

MONTENEGRO ARCHITECTS
SUGARCUBES_page 040

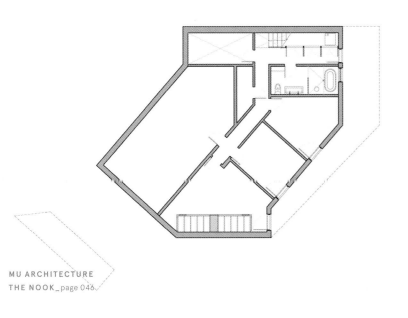

MU ARCHITECTURE
THE NOOK_page 046

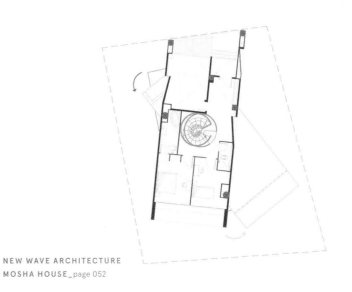

NEW WAVE ARCHITECTURE
MOSHA HOUSE_page 052

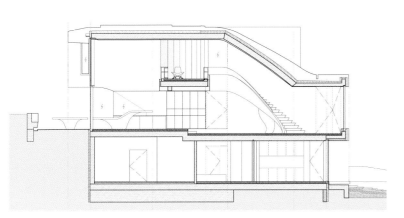

UNSTUDIO
HAUS AM WEINBERG_page 058

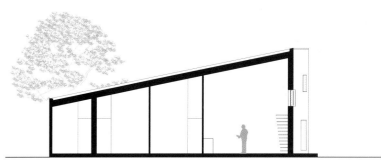

STUDIO RAZAVI
HOUSE FOR A PHOTOGRAPHER_page 064

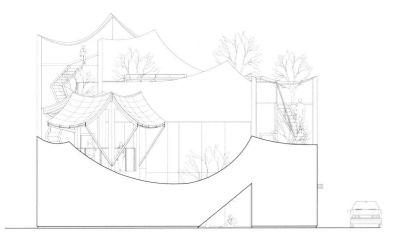

HYOMAN KIM / IROJE KHM
FLYING HOUSE_page 072

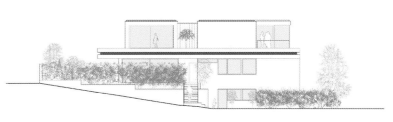

CHRIST. CHRIST. ASSOCIATED ARCHITECTS
S HOUSE_page 078

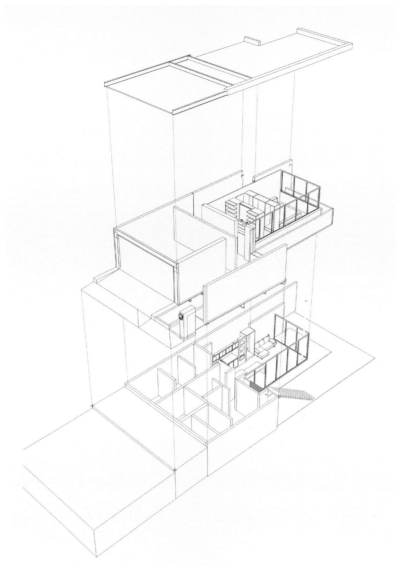

EVELOP ARQUITECTURA
CASA S1_page 084

J. MAYER H. ARCHITECTS
DUPLI.CASA_page 102

MATT GIBSON
SHAKIN' STEVENS HOUSE_page 090

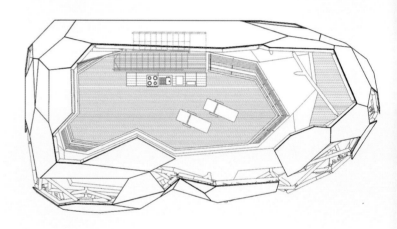

JAKOB + MACFARLANE
CONNECTED HOUSE_page 098

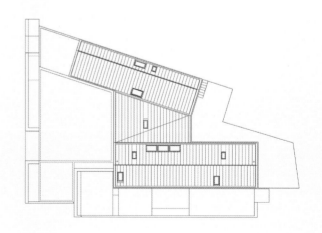

MCGONIGLE MCGRATH
HOUSE AT MAGHERA_page 108

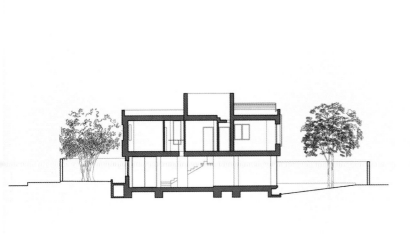

PEDONE WORKING
VILLA DI GIOIA_page 114

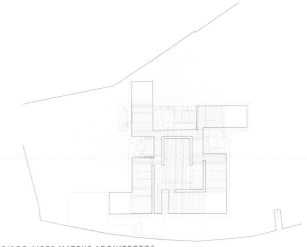

FRANCISCO AIRES MATEUS ARQUITECTOS
HOUSE IN LEIRIA_page 122

CADAVAL & SOLÀ-MORALES
PM HOUSE_page 126

ALBERTO CAMPO BAEZA
CALA HOUSE_page 132

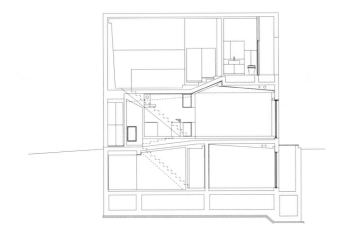

JIN OTAGIRI
GHOST HOUSE_page 138

JFGS ARCHITECTS
GALLARDA HOUSE_page 142

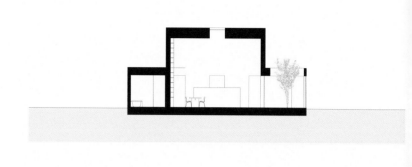

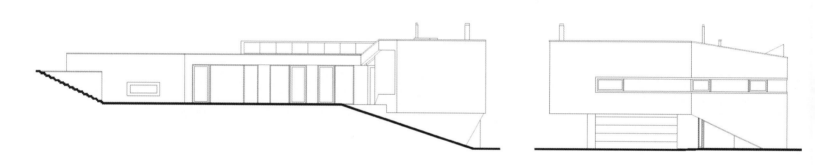

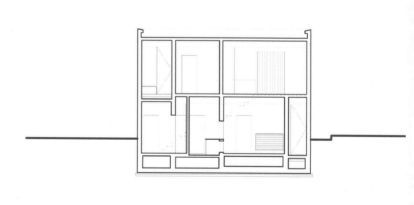

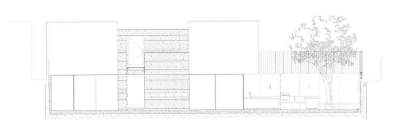

DE MATOS RYAN
GARDEN HOUSE_page 174

DSDHA
COVERT HOUSE_page 182

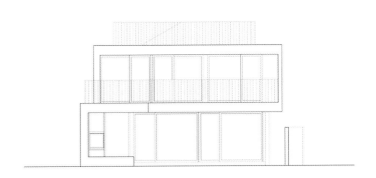

JMY ARCHITECTS
172M2 COMPACT HOUSE_page 190

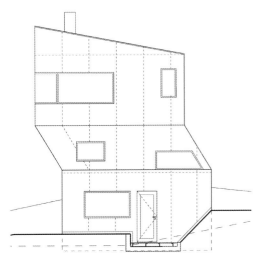

JVA
POLITE HOUSE_page 196

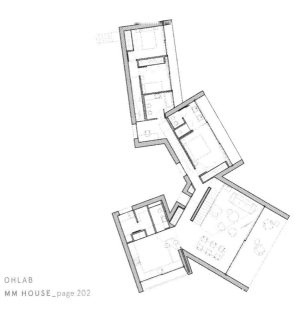

OHLAB
MM HOUSE_page 202

PARASITE STUDIO
C HOUSE_page 208

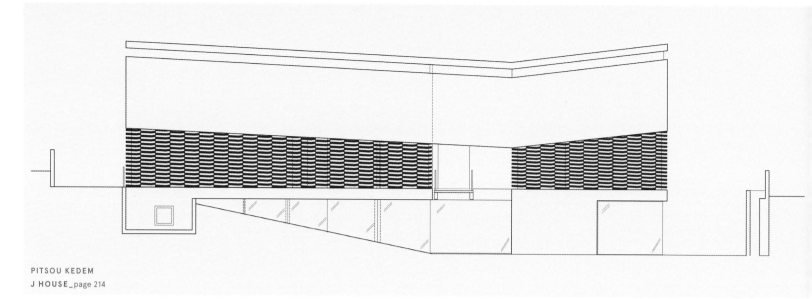

PITSOU KEDEM
J HOUSE_page 214

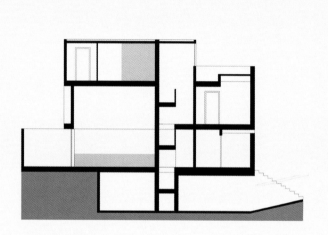

ABRAHAM COTA PAREDES ARQUITECTOS
THE CAVE_page 220

ATELIER TEKUTO
REFLECTION OF
MINERAL_page 226

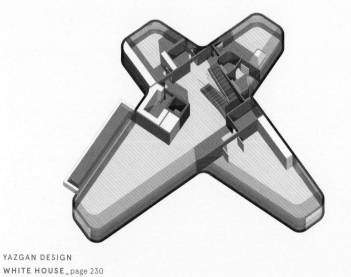

YAZGAN DESIGN
WHITE HOUSE_page 230

314 ARCHITECTURE STUDIO
H3 HOUSE_page 236

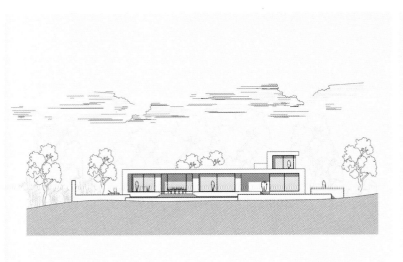

DWEK ARCHITECTURE + PARTNERS
SILVER HOUSE_page 244

KAPSIMALIS ARCHITECTS
SUMMER HOUSE_page 252

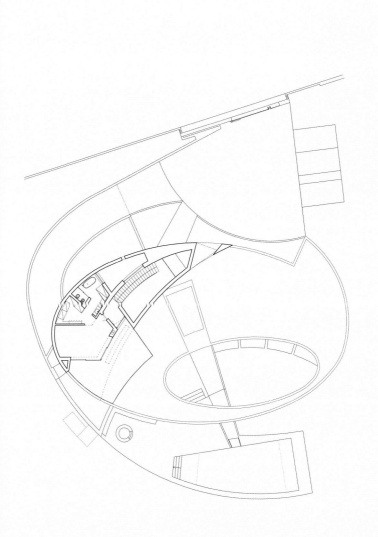

MÁRIO MARTINS ATELIER
CASA ELÍPTICA_page 260

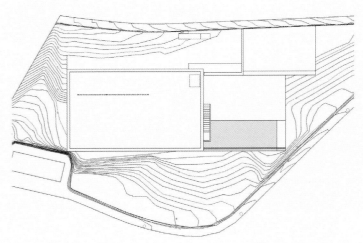

FRAN SILVESTRE ARQUITECTOS
CLIFF HOUSE_page 266

TONKIN LIU
NESS POINT_page 274

314 ARCHITECTURE STUDIO
314architecturestudio.com/mob.php

ABRAHAM COTA PAREDES
ARQUITECTOS
cotaparedes.com

ALBERTO CAMPO BAEZA
campobaeza.com

ATELIER TEKUTO
tekuto.com/en/

CADAVAL & SOLÀ-MORALES
ca-so.com

CHRIST. CHRIST. ASSOCIATED
ARCHITECTS
christ-christ.cc

DELORDINAIRE
delordinaire.com

DE MATOS RYAN
dematosryan.co.uk

DSDHA
dsdha.co.uk

DWEK ARCHITECTURE + PARTNERS
olivierdwek.com

EVELOP ARQUITECTURA
evelop.mx

FRANCISCO AIRES MATEUS
ARQUITECTOS
airesmateus.com

FRAN SILVESTRE ARQUITECTOS
fransilvestrearquitectos.com

HYOMAN KIM / IROJE KHM
irojekhm.com

JAKOB+MACFARLANE
jakobmacfarlane.com

JARMUND/VIGSNÆS JVA
jva.no

JIN OTAGIRI
datar-arch.tumblr.com

J. MAYER H. ARCHITECTS
jmayerh.de

JMY ARCHITECTS
jmy.kr

JOÃO MENDES RIBEIRO
joaomendesribeiro.com

JONAS LINDVALL
jonaslindvall.com

JOSÉ FRANCISCO GARCÍA-SÁNCHEZ
/ JFGS ARCHITECT
jfgs.es

KAPSIMALIS ARCHITECTS
kapsimalisarchitects.com

MÁRIO MARTINS ATELIER
mariomartins.com

MATT GIBSON ARCHITECTURE
+ DESIGN
mattgibson.com.au

MCGONIGLE MCGRATH
mcgoniglemcgrath.com

MONTENEGRO ARCHITECTS
montenegroandpartners.com

MU ARCHITECTURE
architecture-mu.com

NEW WAVE ARCHITECTURE
newwavearchitecture.com

OAB – CARLOS FERRATER
PARTNERSHIP
ferrater.com

OHLAB
ohlab.net

PARASITE STUDIO
parasitestudio.com

PAULÍNY HOVORKA ARCHITEKTI
pha.sk

PEDONE WORKING
pedoneworking.it

PITSOU KEDEM
pitsou.com

RICHARD MEIER & PARTNERS
ARCHITECTS LLP
richardmeier.com

SHINICHI OGAWA & ASSOCIATES
shinichiogawa.com

STUDIO RAZAVI
studiorazavi.com

TAKURO YAMAMOTO ARCHITECTS
takuroyama.jp

TONKIN LIU
tonkinliu.co.uk

TSUKANO ARCHITECT OFFICE
tsukano.jp

UNSTUDIO
unstudio.com

YAZGAN DESIGN
yazgandesign.com

Front cover: Parham Taghioff, Courtesy of New Wave Architecture; Back cover:
© Javiar Callejas; 2: © Serge Anton; 7: © Fernando Guerra / VIEW; 8: Photos: Parham
Taghioff, Courtesy of New Wave Architecture; 9: Photos by José Hevia; 10: Photos by
Sergio Camplone; 12–13: Photos by José Hevia; 14: Montenegro Architects Studio, Ltd;
16–19: Photos by Olivier Blouin; 20–27: © Alejo Bagué; 28–33: © José Campos; 34–39:
Hufton+Crow; 40–45: Montenegro Architects Studio, Ltd; 46–51: © Ulysse Lemerise;
52–57: Parham Taghioff, Courtesy of New Wave Architecture; 58–59: © Iwan Baan /
UNStudio; 60–61: © Christian Richters / UNStudio; 62: © Iwan Baan / UNStudio; 63:
© Christian Richters / UNStudio; 64–69: Photography by Olivier Martin-Gambier; 70:
Sergio Camplone; 72–77: © Sergio Pirrone; 78–83 © Thomas Herrmann; 84–89: Photos by
Andrés Mondragón Padilla; 90–97: © Shannon McGrath; 98–101: © Roland Halbe; 102–107:
© David Franck; 108–113: Aidan McGrath; 114–119: Photos by Sergio Camplone; 120: ©
Javiar Callejas; 122–125: © Fernando Guerra / VIEW; 126–131: © Sandra Pereznieto;
132–136: © Javiar Callejas; 138–141: Photos by Takeshi Yamagishi; 142–144: JFGS /
José Francisco Garcia-Sánchez; 146–151: © Åke E:son Lindman; 152–154: © Shinichi
Ogawa; 156–158: Photos courtesy Pauliny Hovorka; 160–165: © Ken'ichi Suzuki Photo
Studio; 166–171: Photos by Kenichi Asano; 172: © Helene Binet; 174–181: Hufton+Crow;
182–189: © Christoffer Rudquist / DMB; 190–195: ©Yoon, Joonhwan; 196–201: © Lars
Evanger; 202–207: Photos by José Hevia; 208–213: Photography by Wenczel Attila;
214–219: Photography by Amit Geron; 220–225: Photography by Cesar Bejar; 226–229:
Photography by YOSHIDA, Makoto; 230–233: Photography Yunus Özkazanç & Rüya Îpek
Balaban; 234: Photography by Vangelis Paterakis; 236–243: Photos by 314 Architecture;
244–251: © Serge Anton; 252–259: Photography by Vangelis Paterakis; 260–265: ©
Fernando Guerra / VIEW; 266–270: Photos by Diego Opazo; 274–275: Photo by Alex
Peacock; 277: © Edmund Sumner.

On the front cover: Mosha House, Iran,
designed by New Wave Architecture (see page 52).
On the back cover: Cala House, Spain,
designed by Alberto Campo Baeza (see page 132).
Page 2: Silver House, Greece,
designed by Dwek Architecture + Partners (see page 244).

White Houses © 2019 Thames & Hudson Ltd, London
Text by Philip Jodidio
For the illustrations, please see the picture credits list on page 287.

First published in 2019 in the United States of America
by Thames & Hudson Inc., 500 Fifth Avenue, New York,
New York 10110

www.thamesandhudsonusa.com

Library of Congress Control Number 2019932280

ISBN 978-0-500-519837

Printed and bound in China by 1010 Printing International Ltd